Y0-CXM-978

This is a work of historical fiction. Though some names, incidents, and places are authentic and based on actual events, others are the product of the author's imagination.

Summary: After the San Francisco earthquake and fire of 1906, Ernie Bacigalupi and his family are faced with the daunting task of helping others caught in the damaged buildings and refugee camps of the city. Ernie and his father become part of the volunteer firefighting department and play an integral role in rescue efforts.

For Jonathan, Rachel, and Trenton

1

At six-o'clock in the morning, Andrew Bacigalupi got out of bed, checked his pocket watch, and began to wash up for the day ahead. As he shaved his morning stubble with a very sharp straight-edge razor, he looked out the window of his home in the city. San Francisco was teeming with life as usual, and the streets were filled with horses pulling carts and carriages as well as many pedestrians on foot, but almost everyone was work-minded, and that was a pretty safe thing to assume at this time of the morning. During the lovely month of April, the air was cool and inviting as it poured into his open window, but it seemed unseasonably warmer today.

"Thanks for opening the window last night, darling," he said to his loving wife of twelve years. Angelica looked beautiful even in the early morning hours as she rolled over in bed. He loved her very, very much.

"Good morning, sweetheart!" he said to help her get out of bed. Either she didn't hear him, or she was ignoring his voice - hoping to catch a few more winks. As Andrew continued to clean up and get ready for work, she began to finally stir.

"Can you pick up the kids after school and bring them both to the shop with you?" she asked as she sat on the edge of the bed. "You know how Ernie loves to tinker with the broken clocks. You could pick them both up during your afternoon break since the store is so close to school.

"Sure, I'll pick him up right after school is out. If he's going to take over the family business someday, he needs to start learning it soon," said Andrew.

"Don't forget about that new dog we promised them," said Angelica. "We can't go back on our word now, can we? You'd better take some time out on the way to the shop to stop at Ned Furtado's and pick it up. He desperately wants to get rid of the dogs in that litter because he had too many of them, and since he's our friend he said we could have it for free, as long as we give it a good home."

"Sounds great! I'll take care of things this afternoon! I'm sure both of them will be excited to hear the news," said Andrew.

Andrew was the finest watchmaker and clock expert in San Francisco, and he had a very good reputation with his clients. Word of mouth spread quickly, and his business on Mission Street was never hurting for customers. The Bacigalupi clan originated in Genoa, Italy, and Andrew's father Mario was one of the earliest settlers in San Francisco. He did not waste time settling anywhere else, for he knew of the lure of the West. When the Gold Rush was in full swing, he proved to be quite successful with those who gave up on finding their fortune and decided to settle in the city instead. While so many were greedily searching for the mother lode, Mario had kept his wits about him and stuck to what he did best – making fine watches and clocks. He quickly made a fortune within the first few years, and his family reaped the benefits.

"I think I hear Ernie now, banging around in his room," said Angelica. "I'd better get up and make some breakfast for the kids right away. School starts soon, and it takes fifteen minutes just to walk there. It's your turn to walk them and it's right on your way to work. You're so often in a rush to get to work that I end up walking them all the time, and you don't spend enough time with them after school either. Lately you've been coming home around suppertime, and you're missing out on what it means to be a father. You've got to spend more time with them!"

"Yes, yes, Honey, I know. I've been concentrating a lot on the shop to make it successful for us as well as for the children someday. Speaking of breakfast, toast and eggs would sure hit the spot today! Can you make us some?"

"Sure, if it will help you all get a good start today," answered Angelica.

"Thanks, Hon," said Andrew.

As Andrew left the bedroom, Ernie met him in the hallway. Ernie's hair was disheveled as usual in, and his shirt was not buttoned quite right. His twelve-year-old sister, Esther, was already up and just coming out of her bedroom as well.

"Ernie, my boy, you shouldn't rush around so much in the morning that you don't even button up right. You're thirteen now, and you should have such a thing mastered by now," rebuked Andrew.

"I know, Dad, but I have a lot of things on my mind today. Do you know what today is?" asked Ernie.

"Yes, indeed I do, my boy. I believe it is Thursday in the beautiful city of San Francisco, and last time I checked it was 1906," joked his father.

"It's the day we're getting a dog!" shouted a giggling Esther.

"A dog you say? What makes you think you're getting a dog?" asked Andrew.

"Come on, Dad. You know you promised me that we were going to get one today," said Ernie.

"Yes, I know. The Furtados have been trying to get rid of those terriers they have running all over the house for weeks now, so we'll be stopping by after school to get a free dog, and today we'll be walking him to his new home for the very first time. How does that sound?" asked Andrew.

"That sounds great, Dad! I can't wait!" said Ernie, with his sister Esther making similar comments at the same time. After gulping down their breakfast, all three Bacigalupis were ready to head out the door of their beautiful two-story Victorian home on Sutter Street, north of Market. As they were leaving, Andrew picked an orange from one of the many orange trees framing the yard.

"Here's a little snack for your lunch, Esther! Ernie already has one, I think, so I didn't want you to feel left out," said Andrew.

"Thanks, Daddy!" said Esther, popping her orange into the bag lunch she brought for school.

Andrew paused for a minute, taking some time to get a quick glance at the fresh coat of paint he had applied to his home just a few days ago. It really made the rose-colored trim stand out, and he considered himself a lucky man to have such a beautiful home for his family and a great business as well. As they all left for school, he couldn't help but think how hard it would be for both of them to endure a full school day with visions of dogs running through their minds.

2

At last, multiplication problems and reading time were completed, and the hands on the clock at the front of the classroom turned to 3:00 for both Ernie and Esther.

"Class dismissed!" exclaimed Mrs. Mercalli, Ernie's teacher.

"Free at last!" shouted Esther, as she ran out the school doors beside her brother to meet up with her father who was waiting on the sidewalk near the school entrance. Both of them were running at top speed to see who would get there first, and poor Andrew was afraid they were going to knock him over with their youthful and energetic bodies. The sky was bright blue, the air was warm, and all was right with the world as they headed toward the shop.

"Dad, I thought we were going to go to Furtados first today? What happened? Why are we going to the shop?" asked Ernie.

"Well, son, I hadn't been thinking about it much, but Ned Furtado doesn't get home this early. After all, he is a business man too – he's a lawyer. We'll just have to stop over there on the way home. In the meantime, I want to show you and Esther something," said Andrew. "Take a look at what came in today."

"Wow, I never saw one like this before, Dad!" said Ernie.

"Me either," chimed in Esther.

"It's worth a small fortune, you know," said their father.

"It's incredible!" said Ernie as he ran his hands over the fine detailing of the oak grandfather's clock. "Can we get one like this for our house?"

"It probably costs too much, right Daddy?" said Esther.

"Yes, it is expensive, but maybe someday we could get one. But for now, we have other business to tend to. Why don't you both sweep up the shop and then we'll head over to Ned's house," replied Andrew. "Your mother doesn't want us coming home too late."

After about a half hour, the sweeping was done and they headed out the door.

"Mom was saying that this dog is quite something, Dad. She said that terriers were famous for hunting rats back in England, and that the farmers really liked that," said Ernie.

"Is that true, Daddy? Are we getting a rat hunter?" asked Esther.

"Yes, it is true and we are!" said Andrew. "I think we have a few rats at our place, and it won't take long for this dog to track them down."

When they approached the Furtado home, just a few blocks from their own, Andrew took in the view as he so often had when stopping by before. He couldn't begin to imagine how Ned had managed to buy such an expensive and immense Victorian. It was a tri color with bright red trim, a main paint color off-white, and a bright yellow for the decorative framing and other areas. It was easily twice the size of the Bacigalupi home in terms of both lot dimensions and residential square footage, and there was no expense spared when it came to the yard landscaping. Lemon and apricot fruit trees lined the edges of the front yard, with bougainvillea gracefully running up the house columns and many other flowering plants surrounding the trees.

It was quite a sight to see after walking through the busy city – a place bustling with streetcars, horses, buggies, and businessmen on foot wearing fine suits and bowler hats.

"Daddy, is San Francisco the biggest city in the world?" Esther asked.

"Busier than most, but I think New York is bigger yet. You've never seen that, but maybe someday you will," Andrew answered.

As they came up to the front door, Ernie and Esther were almost coming apart at the seams.

"Well, well, well!" said Ned Furtado as he welcomed them in. His grizzly, gray muttonchops were quite distinguishing, and he wore the title of a criminal lawyer well. He was still partially dressed in the suit that he wore at his law firm, and he had come home earlier than usual to meet Andrew and the children. His tie was loose, and his top button unbuttoned.

"Sorry if we are a bit late," said Andrew.

"Not a problem at all, my friend," said Ned. "Glad you made it here with both of the children. From what Mrs. F. told me, Skippy has been running circles around her all day and chasing everything that moves. Killed a rat just last week, and a good guard dog he is as well. His hearing makes him able to hear anyone or anything within fifty yards of the house. But we are willing to give him away to a good home. We don't really need the money, and we know you kids will take good care of him. Besides, our hands are full enough taking care of his mum and pop."

"Thanks a lot, Mr. Furtado!" said Esther. "We will make sure he becomes a good hunter!"

At first, Skippy growled a bit at Ernie when he tried to pet him, and he snarled a bit too, then scampered and hid under the sofa.

"Come on, little guy," coaxed Ernie. "No one is going to hurt you. I've got some beef jerky here in my pocket, and I think you're going to like it!"

"You thought ahead, didn't you, boy?" said Ned. "Don't worry about his snarling. He always does that with strangers. He'll take to you very soon."

"Well, don't worry... we will take good care of him," said Ernie. "I've been waiting for a dog forever, so I'm ready for him. I'll make sure he gets lots of attention."

"Oh, you'll do that alright! He won't have it any other way. You'll have a hard time getting away from him, if I know Skippy! He likes to lay right beside you if you're sleeping or if you're sitting down relaxing. The question is, how much can you take?" asked Ned.

"Oh, I can take it just fine," said Ernie.

"Well, that's enough blabbering now. Let's be on our way, you two!" said Andrew. "I mean, you three!"

"Don't forget his leash Ernie," said Ned. "Enjoy your new dog, kids!"

When they finally arrived home after what seemed like a long walk, with Skippy pulling and tugging every which way on the leash and sometimes being carried, Ernie and Esther were amazed at how many times a dog stops to either mark its territory or to water the bushes. Walking Skippy was definitely an exercise in patience.

"Gosh, Daddy! I don't know how such a small dog can hold so much!" said Esther.

"Well, there are many mysteries of nature, aren't there? It's one of those questions we may never be able to answer very well, Essie," said Andrew.

Skippy was wrapped around a tree in front of their house, and it was odd how he could not find his way around it by reversing his steps and going back the way he came. Intelligence did not seem to be his greatest trait. Esther walked him around the tree to free him, and they all trotted into the house.

"Hey, what took you all so long?" asked Angelica.

"'I will tell you what took so long," answered Esther. "Skippy here had to water every bush in the neighborhood, that's what! But we'll keep him anyway!"

"Mr. Furtado said that he is a good security dog, so no bad guys stand a chance trying to break into our house!" chimed in Ernie.

Skippy started to growl a little at Angelica.

"See what I mean? Just give him some of this jerky and he'll be your friend forever!" said Ernie, as he handed it to his mother.

"Here you go, little guy!" said Angelica. Skippy practically inhaled the treat, and once again a bond was formed.

"Come on now, because supper is ready. I've been making it all day, so you better like it and not complain. I made your favorites –lasagna, fresh salad, and homemade bread!"

Everyone wolfed down the meal, and there was no complaining because it was so good. Ernie and Esther were pretty tired too after walking the dog home and eating a big meal. Skippy was no exception. His food dish was empty, and he drank enough water to sink a ship. After reading from The Adventures of Sherlock Holmes, Ernie went into his bedroom and Skippy followed him and lay down beside him like a good lap dog.

"Hey, I want Skippy in my room tonight!" shouted Esther from the hallway.

"I guess we'll have to take turns," said Ernie. "Don't worry, you'll get to have him in your room later on."

Ernie and Skippy quickly fell asleep on the bed, and the cool San Francisco air poured through an open window, while a distant locomotive added to the sounds of the city.

3

The next morning was a typically cool Tuesday, as the Bacigalupi family was accustomed to. One could always count on the weather in San Francisco to be chilly, foggy, and damp in the morning and a little less that way as the day went on. If you were lucky the sun came out and things warmed up a bit, but that didn't happen very often, especially during the last few weeks. Yesterday's warmth was unusual, and it made the day all the more special.   It seemed like they were having more warm days than usual lately, but that was a welcome change. With fond memories of it all, Ernie's father walked down the hall to his bedroom and drew Skippy from Ernie's bedside.

"Ernie," said his father quietly, trying not to wake the whole family. "It's time to go to work."

Ernie got up out of bed, put on his clothes, and braced himself for another chilly morning of selling newspapers.   There was no time to waste, since he only had a half-hour before breakfast to complete his part time job. It was early, and the rest of the family hadn't gotten up yet, so he figured he would grab his usual breakfast of a piece of toast and a boiled egg when he returned. He brushed his teeth, grabbed his coat from the closet, and made his way to the same street corner where he always stood, every morning for the last two years, the corner of Sutter and Leavenworth.

"Read all about it!" he shouted in his usual style. "Three alarm fire destroys cannery! Fifty-thousand dollars in damage! Enrico Caruso opens Carmen, La Boheme, and Faust! Step right up and get your daily news right here! You sir! How about a paper to start your day off right?"

"Boy, I haven't got time for it right now!" returned a well-dressed businessman in a dark brown wool suit. "Can't you see I'm in a hurry?"

"So sorry, Sir! Maybe tomorrow, eh?" said Ernie in his usual well-rehearsed manner.

"Perhaps!" replied the man hastily.

It was one of those days when Ernie couldn't sell firewood to an Eskimo. So far he only managed to sell about half of his stack, and that was really bad when it came to turning in his tally to the boss. A lot was expected of a young newsy, and he never liked to disappoint, so he turned on the charm even more.

"Good day, Miss!" he said to an attractive young woman who came out of the hotel near his corner. "Surely you want to know what's going on in this magnificent city today, right?"

"Why yes, of course, young man!" replied the woman. She was dressed for success that day, and she seemed ready to face the world. Ernie could usually spot the positive people in a crowd, and he knew whether he would score a sale when judging perspective customers.

"Thank you very much, ma'am!" he said as he handed her the morning edition of The Chronicle.

"I'll take two of those, boy," said another woman, dressed in black with a very fine hat with bright purple plumes. "I like to keep one for my collection and use the other one – I have a wonderful collection of newspapers going all the way back to 1900 and my closet is quite full!"

"Very interesting, ma'am! A bit of a historian, aren't you?" said Ernie, with a big smile on his face.

"Oh yes - indeed I am!" answered the woman. "Working at the library helps me a lot in terms of learning about the past. As you know, we can learn from the mistakes of the past, can't we? That's the wonderful thing about history."

"I'll be sure and drop in sometime and look for you Ma'am, next time I pick up some books," said Ernie.

He was finally getting close to meeting his sales quota now, and he had a few minutes to take in the sights and sounds of the city. He always enjoyed people-watching, and there were people of all sizes and shapes going about their daily business.

He often tried to guess what jobs people had by their clothing choices. Bankers and businessmen always had their suits and ties on, and their fresh shoe-shines plainly evident. People who worked with their hands usually had uniforms on that gave them away – plumbers and carpenters with overalls, food vendors carrying signs and items related to their business, and so on.

What struck him most of all was the way that people were walking down the street. Some followed the rules and stayed on the sidewalks, while others were continually walking in front of horses, carts, and carriages to cross the street anywhere they felt like. It was a wonder that more of them were not hurt or colliding with moving objects such as these. Many of the men especially were racing to get across the street even when the cable cars were very close to them. Ernie guessed that someday he would see headlines telling of the demise of one of these poor souls.

At last his half-hour was up, and he began his quick trip home. Luckily he lived only a few blocks from the corner where he sold newspapers. Within just a few minutes, he was back at home, ready for breakfast, and watching the rest of the family rush around before school.

"There you go, my hard working boy!" said his mother. She placed the toast and the boiled egg before him. Life was good for the Bacigalupis, and little did they know how different their world would become the very next day.

On Wednesday, April the eighteenth, the Bacigalupis, like so many other families in San Francisco, were sleeping soundly in the comfort of their soft beds, when Angelica woke up suddenly with a strange sensation.

"What was that?" she said with a hoarse voice as she leaned forward on her elbows in bed. She didn't know if she was talking to herself or Andrew – it was 5:12 a.m. in the morning. "I think something hit the house... it's shaking!"

The shaking didn't stop but instead became much more violent as it continued. It became clear to both of them that this was no dream and it had nothing to do with the imagination.

"It's an earthquake! Oh, my God!" screamed Angelica. "Quick, get the children! I'll get Esther and you get Ernie!"

Everything in the bedroom was shaking so hard that it sounded like the house was breaking in two. The entire family was in the staircase now, as it too was starting to crumble. Flying glass from a broken mirror, broken plaster, and wood fragments were making it difficult for them to get down the stairs, but everyone made it without being injured by the debris. The quake must have lasted a minute or a minute and thirty seconds.

"What's happening?" screamed Esther.

"No time to talk! Just run!" shouted Ernie. Skippy ran out of the house ahead of them just as the roof was collapsing. The very structure of the house was disintegrating all around them, and it was a race to see if they could make it out before the house itself fell on top of them. Within forty to sixty seconds, there was nothing left of their home except broken fragments of wood, brick, glass, and plaster. It was quite a shock for them to experience all of this at 5:12 in the morning and to be awakened from their sound sleep in such a manner.

The same thing was happening all the way down their street as far as they could tell. Some homes were still standing but hopelessly rocked from their foundations or leaning severely. Families in their bedclothes were standing on sidewalks watching their lives crumble before them. Little did they know the scope of a quake that actually struck an area almost three hundred miles long on the San Andreas fault. How they had escaped in time was an even greater marvel.

"Is this happening all over the city, you think?" asked Mrs. Reed, who lived next door.

"Most likely," said Angelica, with a blank stare. "Andrew! Our home! Our home is gone!" she exclaimed. She then began crying uncontrollably.

Andrew held her close to him as she buried her head in his chest and stood there speechless for a moment. He was in just as much shock. All that he had worked for these past twenty years had gone to pieces. Words could not express what he was feeling at this moment in time. The puzzled look on his face said it all.

After a minute or so, he thought of something he had to do right away.

"Honey, I have to go to the shop at once!

"You can't go now! What are you thinking?" she replied.

"The shop!" he said emphatically. "I have to know for myself whether we have lost all that too!"

"But what will we do in the meantime? Sit on the street in our pajamas and wait for you?" asked Angelica.

"We'll see if we can sift through things before we leave," said Andrew. "Look for clothing and anything still intact that we might be able to save."

After scrounging through the debris that was once their home, the only things they could save were some clothing, a few photo albums, some canned meat, and some other grocery items. Everything else was just too hard to get to. They still had a cart to carry their things on and a horse to pull it.

"Now come with me – both you and the kids," returned the worried father, husband, and businessman. "We'll walk the streets together and see how bad this is, but we've got to get there fast before things get worse."

"Yeah, Mom, we should just go!" said Ernie. "There's nothing we can do here right now."

"What about Skippy? I don't see him anywhere! He was here just a minute ago! I thought I saw him by that bush over there!" shouted Esther. She ran to the bush but couldn't find the terrier anywhere. "He's gone! How will we find him in this mess, Daddy? I know I saw him by the bush, but there is no more house, so how will he know what to do or where to go? We have to stay near here and look for him right away, or we'll never see him again," she cried.

Everyone in the family walked around the demolished home and called for Skippy by name, but they found nothing. Andrew crouched down to his daughter's face level and began to try to convince her of what they had to do next.

"Esther, honey," said Andrew. "I know this is hard for you to understand, but Skippy is just one of our priorities right now. I'm sure we'll find him later, but we will ask Mrs. Reed to keep an eye out for him. Right now, we need to go to the shop and find out if there will be any food for us on the table after this is all over."

"My goodness! Look Andrew! There is almost nothing untouched. Almost every building will have to be torn down," said Angelica.

As their eyes drifted toward the part of town where the shop was, Andrew noticed smoke rising into the air.

"Come with me now, everyone!" ordered Andrew.

It took the four of them about fifteen minutes to get to the shop, since it was just a few blocks from the Bacigalupi home. When they arrived, they saw more smoke coming from the lower floors of the building next to the shop. Firemen had already arrived, since this was one of the first parts of the city to start on fire due to a broken gas leak. Many more of these fires would break out as the day went on, but for now this one took precedence over everyone else who was stranded or wounded. If it wasn't stopped now, it would spread to every block of the city.

As the Bacigalupis approached the store's building complex, Andrew was struck immediately by the speed of the firemen as they hooked up their hoses to the hydrant nearby.

"Chief, the underground water mains are ruptured!" shouted one of the firemen. "We may only have enough water to put this place out. After that, the whole city may go up in flames!"

Indeed, the entire east side of the city was in serious danger. There were only 850,000 gallons of water that would last about five minutes if they were lucky. They would have to put this particular fire out very quickly, or things would really get ugly. A fireman named John Dougherty approached Andrew as the firemen with him finished putting out the fire next to Andrew's shop.

"What are you doing here? Get your family back!" shouted Dougherty.

"This is my shop and my building!" shouted Andrew.

"Well, you're a lucky man then," said Dougherty. "It looks like we have saved this one, but the rest of the east half is in serious trouble! God help us all! Where is Chief Sullivan when we need him?"

Little did Dougherty know at that moment that his boss, the well-respected fire chief, Dennis Sullivan, was lying mortally wounded under a pile of debris at the California Hotel. A cupola had crashed through his apartment ceiling, and he had not even the slightest chance of escape.

"As far as the rest of the city goes, we've got two possible solutions!" shouted Dougherty to the other firemen. "We might be able to use the reserves in those ancient cisterns below the streets, but they are so old that they may not work!

If that fails, we could suck some of that seawater out of the bay! That may be our best shot!"

Both of these strategies would indeed take forever, and time was a luxury that they did not have. Gas lines were rupturing all over the city, and buildings were beginning to blow up in most of the business district. There were no working fire alarms or telephone systems. Communication had broken down to the point that things looked hopeless.

"Angelica, it looks like we may have something left of the shop, but with the rest of the city being in a shambles, that won't do us much good," said Andrew. "We simply have to find a place for the kids to stay. We can't keep dragging theme all over the place as the city is crumbling before our eyes, and it's too dangerous! Let's go to your parents' place. Maybe by living on the outskirts of town, they have been spared from all this."

So the four of them began their long journey to Franklin Street in the Western Addition, where Angelica's father and mother lived in another Victorian, even bigger than Andrew's. It was hard to tell where they were because the buildings were so demolished that there was very little left of them. Now and then they would recognize buildings that they passed, and they made their way the best they could around the debris.

"Dad, look!" shouted Esther. "There's a big crack in the street!"

They approached the area where a deep, deep trench had been created by the earthquake, and they did their best to find a narrow area where they could leap over it.

"Be careful, Andrew! Hold on to your papa, Esther," said Angelica with as calm a voice as she could muster. Though the crack in the brick road was only a foot apart, the depth of it was the most frightening part.

"Okay, I'm across now, so just hold my hand, Honey, and you'll be fine," said Andrew.

Andrew took her hand in his gently and pulled her over the deep, dark trench. He knew Ernie would have no problem jumping it, but he wanted to make extra sure that he was not going to fall in.

"Now Ernie, I know you can get over this just fine, but hold my hand anyway just for a little extra security," said Andrew.

"Okay, Dad. It is pretty deep," replied Ernie. With that they were over the danger and ready to journey on. They knew it was a long trip, and they desperately wanted to get there before dark and make sure that the grandparents were not harmed. After walking through the ruins of the city and seeing houses starting to set each other on fire, they were very much hoping to see some sense of normalcy as they pushed on. Gradually, they did begin to notice less damage as they approached the West Addition near O'Farrell and Franklin.

"Oh my, what a relief to see that some people didn't have to go through what we did!" said Angelica, as she looked at the neat and tidy homes so well painted and landscaped. There was something so strange about it all, going from ruins to normal life again, but it was a welcome change, and she knew it meant that her parents were probably unhurt.

They all walked up to the front door after walking many miles, sore and tired.

"Aren't you all a sight for sore eyes!" said Grandma Barton. "You're all okay! Thank the Lord!" she said, with tears streaming down her face. Grandpa Barton approached and gave each member of his family a huge hug, smiling from ear to ear, with the wrinkles on his face even more visible than before.

"Oh Mama, we are so glad to see that you are safe too! We couldn't use the telephones and there was no way to know anything about what was going on everywhere else," said Angelica.

"Well, we may not be safe ourselves. Houses are burning up one after another to the south of us. They say somebody was cooking ham and eggs when her chimney flue was broken from the quake, and a fire started in her wall. From there it started spreading all over the neighborhood. For the meantime, we are okay. Fill us in on what happened, and we'll get you some food right away," said Grandma Barton. The four of them sat in the living room and talked over the events of the day.

"We basically lost everything," said Angelica, weeping a little herself at the thought of it all. She had managed to control her emotions pretty well until seeing her parents, and then everything just poured out of her. "Our home is gone, and so is our whole neighborhood."

"And so far the shop is safe," said Andrew. "The place next door was on fire, but the firemen managed to put it out before it got to the store. Now if only they can put out any other fires that start, we should be in the clear, but that is a big if."

"Well, some things are out of our control, aren't they, Son?" said Grandpa Barton. "You'll all just stay with us until we figure out what to do next. What other choice is there? God was gracious enough to spare us and our home, when so many others lost theirs."

"But what about Skippy, Dad?" said Ernie. "We've got to find him before it is too late!"

"Son, don't forget what I told you before. We've got bigger things to think about, but I'm going to eat something, and then maybe head back out there and see what I can do. I'm going alone, though, because we can't keep putting you two in danger," he said to the children. "There is still quite a bit of daylight left. "

It was about two-thirty in the afternoon as they sat down to have some soup that Grandma had made for the evening meal. After all that they had endured, the delicious vegetable soup really helped them calm down and get some strength back. They also ate some fresh bread and drank a big glass of milk to finish off the meal. It was so nice to be free of all the madness for a little while.

After the meal, Andrew sat down with his wife to figure out a plan for the rest of the day. He knew he had to do something to help out, but he wasn't sure where to start. All that he knew was that he had to do it alone, without jeopardizing the safety of his family.

"Look, Daddy," said Esther. "There's smoke!" As he looked out the window, the fires in the city were spreading even more than he could have ever imagined. The sky was beginning to turn a reddish-gray, ominous looking color as the smoke continued to rise.

"Listen, honey, I'm going to start walking back to the city, now that the children are safe here with your parents, said Andrew. "I can't just sit here in comfort while I know so many people are out there and in serious trouble. Maybe I can find Skippy too by some miracle."

"But Andrew, what if something happens to you? What will I do then?" asked Angelica.

"I'll be careful, Angie, and I'll try not to do anything stupid. I've got you and the kids to think about," replied Andrew.

As Andrew left the house, he could not believe how this small patch of homes had somehow escaped damage. Somehow the house of his in-laws was unscathed, like a virtual island in a sea of sharks. People continued to wander around aimlessly with no real place to go. Fires were burning everywhere and the air was filled with smoke. There was an eerie glow above the whole city. Shelters had been organized for some in what was left of nearby churches, but even most of the churches had taken on serious foundation damage. Almost every building seemed to be knocked cockeyed on its footing or burning to the ground. Roofs had sunken in, walls were leaning, and chimneys were crumbling. One home he passed had no walls left at all. In some parts of the city there were even charred corpses of people who had tried to escape the fires but failed. Even policemen were shooting people who were looting various businesses. The world seemed to be falling apart. He had to try to think clearly in the midst of all the chaos.

"Where should I go first?" Andrew said out loud to himself. Suddenly, Andrew thought he heard the sound of a child's voice. It was hard to make out above the noise on the street, but as he followed the sound he came to one of the homes on his block that had three of the four walls still intact. Somehow the fires had not yet reached it. He continued tracking the child's moaning and started to think it was a young girl's voice.

"Hello, can you hear me?" shouted Andrew as he looked inside the shambles of a home. "Are you alright?"

"I think my leg is broken!" came the girl's reply. "It hurts so much! Please help!"

As Andrew lifted the broken boards and sifted through the debris, he finally saw the arm of the girl. He continued his careful removal of the debris around it until her head and shoulders were finally exposed. She looked to be about ten, and there were scratches and lacerations all over her neck and shoulders, but there appeared to be nothing seriously injured above her waist.

"I'm going to lift these boards off your leg now, but it may hurt when I do it. I'll try to be as careful as I can. What's your name, dear?" asked Andrew.

"Jenny," replied the girl. She was wearing a set of pajamas yet, obviously awakened during her sleep like everyone else.

"Tell me, Jenny. Is there anyone else in your family we should look for? Did you hear your family leave by any chance?" asked Andrew.

"I don't know...I think I was not awake if they did leave. My mother was making breakfast for my dad, who gets up really early, and that was the last thing I heard before the house fell on top of me. I don't know where she is. It's just my parents and me. I don't have any brothers or sisters," answered the girl.

By the look of things, Jenny's parents were no longer alive, but Andrew couldn't be sure of that. What was left of the house was shrouded in total silence, and the fires were sure to reach them soon.

"I'm going to see if I can come up with a plan to protect that leg of yours and get you out of here," said Andrew.

He managed to pull her out of the rubble, and set her down on the ground. She moaned in pain, and Andrew surmised that her leg was most likely fractured, as there was no bend in it. Tying a small board to Jenny's leg, he then used some cloth that he had torn from his shirt to make a splint and sat down to think for a minute.

"What are we going to do now?" mumbled Andrew to himself. "Maybe there is someone around here with a horse and buggy who could give us a lift. Let's just wait here a while and see what happens."

"You know, after all of this, I still don't know your name," said Jenny.

"Andrew... Andrew Bacigalupi. Pleased to meet you, Jenny. If we can just get some help from someone, we can get a search party out to look for your parents, but right now, things aren't looking so good, I'm afraid. The firemen are all running around like they can't do a thing, and many people are too busy worrying about themselves to help anybody, but wait we will."

About a half-hour later, a policeman finally showed up. "Looks like you've got a problem here too," he said with a sense of exhaustion in his voice. "The whole city is in an uproar, but I couldn't just ignore a little girl like you in distress, now, could I?" How bad is that leg of yours, dearie?" asked the policeman.

"It hurts really bad! I don't know what happened, but it's much worse now than it was a while ago," moaned Jenny.

"I suppose it's starting to swell a bit right now. No way of knowing just how bad it is without a doctor looking at it. But it was real smart to wrap it up like you did!" said the policeman.

"That was Mr. Bacigalupi who did that," said Jenny.

"Well, Mister, that was real kind of you to help this litle lady, but I think you'd be wise to head on back to your own family and your own troubles. I'll take care of Jenny, here, and thank you for your help, sir! It was a noble thing to do," said the officer.

"Goodbye, Jenny. It looks like you are in good hands now. I'm glad I could help. It beats wandering around feeling helpless. Hopefully, I can find my kid's little pouch too," said Andrew, bidding them farewell.

So Andrew continued on his way, toward the area where his house once stood tall. It was hard to tell exactly where he was, but there were still a few landmarks left behind to help him somewhat. He crossed many streets and took shortcuts through the rubble to get there faster. Homes were burning, walls were caving in, and smoke continued to blanket the sky wherever he looked. Bodies were lying covered up on the streets, and it looked like there was going to have to be a mass burial site as more were pulled from the damaged buildings. His brief moment of glory was now over, but helping the little girl had been therapeutic for him when so much death was around every corner.

As Andrew got nearer to his own street again, he noticed that his own home had burned completely to the ground. He knew there was no saving it anymore, but it looked like the street where his friend Antonio lived had not yet caught fire. As he approached the home, he hoped for signs of life.

"Antonio! Are you and your family okay?" he called.

As Andrew peered through the wreckage, there was no sign of Antonio Ferrante or his family. He walked carefully through the tumbled down walls and splintered wood and so no life whatsoever. Perhaps they had gotten away in time and gone elsewhere, or maybe they were all dead. He searched everywhere in hopes of finding them and their three children. Just babies they were – two, four, and six years of age. He took it as a good sign that no bodies were to be seen. It was highly unlikely that all of them had died, so he concluded that they all must have gotten away somehow beforehand.

"Well, I guess there is no more to be done here," mumbled Andrew to himself. As he lifted a board to clear his path toward the next room, he noticed something strange. It looked as though there was some brown hair poking out from under the plaster pieces that had once been living room walls. The hair seemed to be moving, ever so slightly.

"Oh, dear Lord! I hope that's not human hair!" shrieked Andrew. He got up closer to it and knelt down. Picking up the plaster piece, he discovered something both shocking and amazing. "Skippy! I can't believe you made it, little buddy! Who would have ever guessed I'd see you again! You're still alive and kicking! Oh, my, the kids are not going to believe this! You must have run in here at just the wrong time and gotten trapped! But are you okay, little guy?" Andrew shouted.

As he examined the little terrier, Andrew quickly ascertained that there were no broken bones or serious injuries. Miraculously, the little tyke had just been trapped beneath the plaster walls and unable to get out. However, he did notice that once Skippy was freed he did have some trouble moving a little. He had been weakened severely by the shock of it all and by the weight of the debris, and he was very dehydrated as well.

He took the little pup in his arms and carried him back into the street. He couldn't help but wonder whether the Ferrantes were alright or not. There was far too much turmoil going on throughout the city to do much of any thinking at all about it. He headed for his own lot, hoping to find some answers rather than questions. At least now he had the dog back, and Ernie and Esther would be able to rest easy about that. He knew the importance of pets to children, especially during times of crisis such as these.

As he entered the remains of what was once his beautiful Victorian home, Andrew was sure that there was no hope of saving it. The place had been completely lifted off its foundation and was no longer structurally sound. He slumped in a corner of what was once his bedroom and began to cry. He was not sure why he had come here. For some reason he was drawn to it, though he knew how hopeless it all was.

"Well, my little friend," he said to Skippy. "It's time we got back to Ernie and Esther with some good news. Let's get out of this confounded mess and go back to Grandpa's home where there is still a roof over our heads."

"Skippy!" shouted Ernie as he saw his father carry him inside. "I can't believe it! Where was he, Dad?

"Somehow he had wandered over to the Ferrante place," said Andrew. "I don't know how a dog his size managed to stay alive in that mess, with the house falling in on him and all, but he made it out alive!"

"Skippy must have had angels watching over him," said Angelica, as she and Esther entered the room. Esther was quick to pick up her little dog and hug it to pieces when she saw it.

"What else happened out there, Andrew?" asked Angelica.

"Well, I found a little girl named Jenny in a demolished house over on Bush Street. Luckily, the police were not too far away and they came to the rescue. There must be thousands of people like her in this city, and a thousand more that are worse off, but by some stroke of luck, we managed to have a policeman walk right by us," answered her husband.

Just then there was a knock on the door. Andrew went to see who it was.

"Andrew, my good man! You're a sight for sore eyes! I saw your house burned down and started to think the worst!" said Ned Furtado, their old friend and dog donor.

"Well, we are alive alright, and the store is intact yet as far as I know, but the buildings around it caught fire from the winds, and that started a chain reaction throughout the city," said Andrew.

"But we got Skippy back!" shouted Esther.

"You mean you lost him?" said Ned.

"Just 'til Daddy could find him!" she said.

"Well, I am sure glad of that, little girl! You can't go losing him when you just got him now, can you?" said Ned kindly.

"Daddy, will we ever get to see our house fixed up? We can fix it, right?" said Esther. She was a master at changing the topic of conversation. "I miss our house!" she said as she played with some dolls.

"Honey, we are probably going to have to live either here or at Daddy's store until we can build a new house," answered Andrew patiently. "It's going to be okay though. There is plenty of room upstairs at the shop to set up a bedroom or two. Don't you worry about it, at least for now. We are going to be just fine!" said Andrew.

"Well, you probably are wondering why I came here, Andrew," said Ned, changing the conversation once again. "I knew that your parents lived here, and as I was checking out the damage in our neighborhood, there were firemen everywhere asking for help. They really need some volunteer firemen right now, Andrew, and with the holocaust that is going on there is not much time to organize a volunteer fire department."

"But where do we start? What do we do, just jump into a flaming building?" came Andrew's sarcastic reply.

"The last thing I heard, the Emporium area was the worst, so let's hitch a ride with somebody and head over there. Maybe they can give us protective fire suits to wear and some equipment as well. If not, we'll just do whatever we can. I know it's been a long day for you already, so rest a bit and then we'll head out, okay?" said Ned.

"Well, it beats just sitting here waiting for the fire to spread and come over this way, doesn't it Angie?" said Andrew.

"Yes, honey. But do rest just a few minutes first, and again, be careful!" said Angelica. "You can do some good out there instead of just sitting here, and I'll stay with the kids and Skippy to keep him from getting lost again."

"Dad, can I go with you?" said Ernie. "I'll bet I could help out somehow. There is nothing to do here anyway!"

"Not on your life, Ern! It is far too dangerous! You and Esther are needed more here to keep your mum from worrying and to take care of Skippy. Don't let him out of your sight this time, because I'm not going out looking for him again!" warned Andrew.

"Yes, Ernie! Stay here and play with me," said Esther. "Please don't go!"

"Trust me, Essie, he's not going anywhere!" said their father.

"But Dad, I don't know how long I can just sit here watch what's going on out there! There must be something I can do!" said Ernie.

"For now, you can stop your old man from worrying! Let's go, Ned!" said Andrew.

Andrew gave his wife a gentle kiss and a huge hug to each of the children, grabbed his coat, and grabbed an ax that belonged to his father-in-law. The two men then headed out the door in search of the unknown.

7

As the fire continued to spread near the Emporium, the firemen were desperate in their attempt to contain it. John Dougherty, the hastily appointed replacement for Fire Chief Dennis Sullivan, felt helpless to face the disaster before him. He had very little experience or know-how to confront it all, and even Sullivan himself would have been hard-pressed to do so.

"What are we going to do, boys?" shouted Dougherty above the noise of the street where things were going up in flames. His men were as dumbfounded as he was. "We can't stop this wind from blowing and we can't slow down the flames no matter how hard we try. Our water is gone, and there seems to be no way to get any. It's like trying to stop a twister from blowing at you by hiding behind an umbrella!"

"So what happened to the plan for getting water from the cisterns or by the bay?" said his second in command, Ben Williams.

"Not going to happen! There are no people or resources to do it! Nobody expected a disaster of this magnitude. There was no Plan B!" shouted Dougherty again. Dougherty's former boss, Chief Sullivan, had warned the city many times that such a fire would soon happen, since the city had already endured a total of five major fires in the last few decades, but no one in governmental circles was willing to spend the money on such things.

"Our only hope is to get some dynamite and blow up some of those ruined buildings to create a firebreak. It just might stop it all from spreading further. Although I've n ever used such a drastic method, it's the only card we have left to play!" answered Dougherty.

"I think you're right, Chief! The navy's not sending us water from the bay, and frankly, I don't know how we can even make that all happen!" replied Williams.

"That's it, Ben! We have no other options. We'll have to send for help from the Presidio to get that dynamite over here fast! God help us all!" screamed the fire chief over the noise of the blazing buildings.

At that moment, Chief Dougherty was abruptly interrupted by Ned Furtado and Andrew, who had just rode up on a stranger's buggy. People in the city were more helpful than usual under such circumstances, and they had quickly hitched a ride with a kind old man and his wife, who were on their way to the tent city that had been set up at the Presidio.

"Excuse me, sir!" said Ned. "Are you in charge here?"

"Dougherty's the name. Yes, I am in charge, but I'm awful busy right now, friend. No time to talk!"

"Sir, just a minute of your time, and then we'll be off if you want. We've come to help. Consider us your volunteer fire department. You can't say you don't need help now, can you?" said Andrew.

"Know anything about explosives?" asked Dougherty. "We plan to use some to create a firebreak in the city streets, and we need some men to help us load it up. I'm sure we can use you after that, too!"

Ned took Andrew aside for a moment to consider this.

"I don't think Angie or my wife would be too anxious for us to go this far, Andrew!" said Ned.

"Who's to say she has to know?" said Andrew. "If this is how we are helping, so be it! We don't have time to hesitate. It's now or never!"

"Okay, Chief! We are in! Where do we start?" said Ned.

"Get in that wagon! It's headed for the Presidio to pick up fifty cases of dynamite. You're going to get it, and you're bringing it back too - carefully!" shouted the fire chief. "I'll send some men with you to help load up. Now get going! We need a lot of firepower!" said the chief.

8

As they passed nearly every street, the blocks were a raging inferno. The fire took on its own monster-like quality, a demon to be conquered by a small band of men. Dougherty hardly knew where to start, but he was sitting on a huge pile of dynamite, and it was now or never. Andrew and Ned were riding in the back of the wagon, and their job was to unload the dynamite as quickly as possible.

"Hand me that case, Ned," said Andrew. "Come on! Speed it up before it's too late!"

Dougherty and his men began planting the explosives in the basements of the buildings at the edge of the firebreak. If they could blow up the old mission and the surrounding buildings before they burst into flames, they might keep the fire from spreading. It was their only hope for saving the part of the city that was still untouched.

"Andrew, it looks like we're going to need your help to plant these remaining explosives," shouted Dougherty, as flames engulfed the building behind them. "Be careful of the wire! Don't let it get caught in anything, or the entire case will be wasted!"

Ned and Andrew ran with the cases of dynamite in their hands. It was difficult if not impossible to see where they were going because of the thick smoke that permeated their lungs. They ran into the mission building and found the basement. Everything seemed strangely quiet after all the noise in the street as they quickly began to string out the explosives as far as they would reach and then went back for more. This happened about a dozen times in rapid succession, and their bodies were riddled with exhaustion and sweat. Finally, the job was completed.

"Looks good, Andrew!" shouted Ned. "Well done! Now let's get out of here before the whole place is blown to kingdom come!"

"Yeah, run for it, Ned!" screamed Andrew above the crashing sounds of buildings nearby that were collapsing in the flames. "I hope there's not some trigger- happy fool on the end of this wire!"

No sooner had Andrew made his point when suddenly the dynamite began to go off. The two men weren't even halfway to the entrance when ceilings began to cave in and gas lines ruptured and exploded. Ned was the first to be trapped by a fallen floor joist that was splintered badly and weighing down heavily on his legs.

"Ned, are you alright?" shouted Andrew from underneath a huge pile of rubble. Unlike Ned, Andrew was able to crawl out from under the debris just in time to avoid being crushed by it, but both of them were hopelessly trapped within the area that had blown up prematurely. The entire building was on top of them, and there was barely room to move in the tight, small space where they found themselves confined. A horrible groan came from beneath the wood and cement that had obliterated the view of Ned's lower body.

"I'm alive…" squeaked Ned's weak voice. "I can't move my legs at all, and I can't feel them either. This doesn't look good, Andy."

"Maybe I can help you get free," said Andrew. "I don't know if I can move that beam though. It's a lot bigger than I am, but where there is a will, there's a way." As he pushed and pulled at the beam, he realized that it was just no use trying anymore.

"They should come looking for us, right?" questioned Ned.

"Hopefully, but they may just be too busy stopping the city from burning at the moment. I'm afraid all we can do is wait and see, and don't forget to pray," answered Andrew.

An hour went by as they screamed and waited for help, but none proved to be nearby. The others must have been busy either putting out fires or planting more explosives, since they heard a lot of explosions from other parts of the building. Other firemen shouting and yelling out orders could be heard in the distance, but the voices were faint and barely audible.

"Ned, we're not getting anywhere this way, and those legs of yours need attention soon. I think I'd better go and find a medic or something. I can't just stay here with you, buddy. So stay strong, pray hard, and I'll be back with someone to help. Just stay still and don't move, and I think you will be alright for the time being. "Goodbye, my friend, and God be with you till we meet again!"

"Oh Lord, please help me now," prayed Ned. "I know I haven't always been the man you want me to be, but I promise that if you can get me through this, I will dedicate my life to you in a big way. Please be with the others in harm's way right now, and forgive my sins. If it is time for me to enter your kingdom, I am ready." With that Ned trailed off into a deep sleep.

Meanwhile, back at 8th Street and Market, where the building being demolished was located, Chief Dougherty was in a quandary about what to do next. At this point, most of the building that housed the old mission was gone, and the fire seemed to be in check. It was not spreading further, and he was about to tell his men to pack up and leave for other places when another fire broke out in the neighborhood of Gough and Hayes. It was now 10 a.m., and the day was just beginning.

"What in God's name started this fire now?" he shouted to George McIntyre, one of his officers. "What's the latest on our water situation, McIntyre? Do we have anything left anywhere to put this new fire out?"

"Sir, from the latest reports, we don't have the slightest water left. The 850,000 gallons we had were all used up in five minutes, and it looks like we have no choice but to watch the city burn. I'm sorry, sir, and I wish I had better news. We just weren't prepared for something of this magnitude, and I don't think any fire department ever could be."

As they watched the fire spread, it was indeed wiping out the entire Mission District and the Hayes Valley section. The mission building that Ned was trapped in was gone, but it had actually created a huge avenue for the fire to spread. Buildings that might have served as firebreaks were wrecked, but worst of all was the flaming debris that had ignited the gas lines throughout the city. The fire department, the mayor, and the army were all busy blaming each other as the calamity grew, repeating the confusion that seemed to rule over the fire itself. No one knew what to do.

"Chief! Chief!" screamed Andrew in agony as he crawled from the rubble of the building. It had taken every ounce of strength he had left to crawl through very small openings, jagged glass, cement fragments, and every other kind of hazard known to man.

"It's Ned! He's alive! He is still in there, and his legs are badly hurt underneath a huge pile of debris. I tried to free him, but it was no use. Can you send some men down there? Are there any medics who can help? We've got to do something!" reported Andrew.

"Of course we will do what we can, Andrew. Your courage and sense of duty today was very admirable. I will be sure to report this to my superiors - what you men did for this city today. I'll get a man or two on it, but we will need most of them to go looking for whatever people we can save without water hoses. We are in a heap of trouble right now, and we have very few support services. I'm sure whatever medics we have are busy too."

"Well, I am going to go back to my family now and see how they are doing. A man has to make priorities during times like this, and family is one of them." With that, Andrew made his way back to his grandparents' home, one of the few buildings left standing. As he did so, his son Ernie had been busy making plans of his own.

"Sneaking out of the house when no one was looking was the only way we could go help, huh Skip?" he said to his faithful dog. "I know they'll be worried about me, but I'd never get a chance to do anything if I didn't make some plans myself," he continued.

Ernie and Skippy had actually followed his father all the way to the mission building without being seen, and Ernie had been listening in on all the conversations between Andrew and Chief Dougherty. He knew Ned was trapped in the lower regions of the building, and he and Skippy were just the ones to help out in such an emergency. Everyone seemed to have given up on poor Ned. McIntyre and his fellow officer tried to get through the debris, but had no luck whatsoever, and they quickly reported to their chief that it was too late for poor old Ned. It was a good thing that he had been watching the whole thing from a slight distance, around the corner, because he knew now just where to go in.

"I know this is dangerous, little buddy," said Ernie, but we've got to try! We can't just leave poor old Ned there to die!"

And so they made their way through the small opening from which Andrew had emerged. The air was thick with dust and there were sharp pieces of steel and wood pointing every which way. It was a true wonder that his dad had ever gotten through it, because it was even a tight tunnel for him and Skippy. They creeped and crawled through the tiny spaces for what seemed like an hour, though it was only fifteen minutes. As they proceeded to climb over the mess, Ernie continued calling Ned's name, but there was no response.

"Where in the world is he?" said Ernie to himself. "Can it be much further? Why doesn't he answer?" He was indeed starting to think it was too late, when he heard a faint voice about ten feet from him.

"Ernie? Is that you?" said the weak and frail voice.

"Yes, Mr. Furtado! It's me! I was starting to give up on you there for a second!" shouted Ernie as he crawled over to see what the situation was.

"It doesn't look good, Ern!" said Ned. "I think there is just too much stuff on top of me to crawl out. Whatever is left of my legs can't be good. It might make it worse if you save me. You've got to get out of here, now, and just let me go. It's better this way, and I'm ready for it. The building could start to collapse on you anytime, and I'm a goner anyway."

"Just stop talking like that, Mister F, because you know I'm not going to leave here without giving it a try! I'm going to just take this stuff off of you one piece at a time, if it takes me all day!"

With that, Ernie began to remove cement pieces and wood fragments as best he could. He couldn't move all of it, but he knew that if he moved some of it, that might be all that was needed. He worked carefully so as to avoid causing more to fall down, and Skippy had begun digging underneath Ned.

"What are you doing, boy?" said Ernie. "You're a terrier all right! Good for digging out rats and other small rodents. You make me proud, Skip! Way to go, little guy!"

Actually, what Skippy was doing gave Ernie a great idea. He had found a shovel outside the building that had been forgotten by McIntyre and his companion, and he knew it might come in handy for rescuing Ned. He too, began to follow Skippy's lead and dig underneath poor Ned.

"What would I do without you, Ernie!? You're doing what grown men could not do, and I think it's going to work! Keep digging and we just might all make it out of here."

And so he did. Ernie dug and dug until he could dig no more. At the near point of exhaustion, he realized that Ned could now move his legs. Little by little, he was indeed edging his way from the debris, and Skippy moved out of the way just in time to keep from being sat on.

"Yes! You've done it Ernie! It looks like only one of my legs is broken, and I think the other one is going to be alright!"

"That's great, Mr. F! Way to go, Skip! Between the two of us, it worked! But we've got to do something to support that leg! I know! I'll tear off one of my shirt sleeves, and then I'll tie it around your leg and this piece of wood here as a brace. There, that should do it! Okay, Mr. F., it is now or never! It's time to get you out of here!"

Ernie, Skippy, and Mr. Furtado then made their way through the tiny passageway that was still clear for an escape. It was much harder of course, with Ned hardly having enough strength to pull himself along, but together they managed to pull it off. Ernie had to grab him by the arms on many occasions to do it, but they finally made it out.

Just as they were emerging, there they saw Andrew. He had had second thoughts about leaving poor Ned there, and had turned around while he was about half-way home. Little did he know that his son had left home and gone to rescue Mr. Furtado from a near death. He had lost a good deal of blood, and help of some kind was sorely needed to slow the whole process down.

"Do my eyes deceive me? I must be dreaming or seeing a mirage!" shouted Andrew. He rubbed his eyes in disbelief as he took in the scene. There was his own son, dragging Ned across the ground while Skippy tagged along barking and running circles around them both.

"Can you believe it, Dad? Skippy and I got him out! It's a miracle!" shouted Ernie, panting from all the exercise he had gotten.

"What kind of shape is that leg in, Ned? Let's have a look," answered Andrew.

"It's broken alright, but I'm going to live! If Ernie hadn't come along, I wasn't so sure about that!" said Ned. "Skippy did his part too – that is one heck of a dog!"

"Well, for now we need to figure out how to get you to safety and to a doctor." The three of them waited a while there by the demolished building as the fires roared all around. Finally a steam engine arrived with a few men on it. "Quick, men! We've got an injured man here and he needs a lift."

The men on the steam engine loaded Ned in and brought him to the makeshift hospital inside some tents that had been set up about nine city blocks away. The wounded inside were in terrible shape, with many of them moaning and bleeding and shaking with pain. They put Ned on a stretcher and set him down for some medical attention, but it would be a while before they could get to him.

"You should both get back now, Andrew! I'll be okay now that I am here. Just get that boy home before he does something else crazy, and Ernie, don't lose that dog! He's a keeper!"

10

After getting back to Ernie's grandparents' home, Ernie got to share the whole story of how he and Skippy got to save Mr. Furtado from being trapped for a very long time. During the meal, his parents had more than a few comments regarding the whole situation.

"Ernie, though we are really proud of you for saving Mr. Furtado, we also want to remind you that you could have been seriously hurt while going in that building. It was a crazy thing to do, and you need to stop taking such chances right away!" said Andrew, in the most authoritative voice he could manage.

"But Dad, I couldn't just sit here while I knew so many people were in trouble. I just wanted to help, and if I hadn't, who knows what would have happened to Mr. F." replied Ernie.

"We know that, Ernie, but we need you to do these things with parent supervision, and that is all there is to it!" answered Angelica firmly. "You will not be leaving this house for the next twenty four hours at least, and we are locking your room if we have to go away. Extraordinary times call for extraordinary measures, young man."

Wanting to change the direction this conversation was going, Ernie decided to talk about something else. "Did you hear about the tents that they are setting up in the Presidio? While I was on my way to help Mr. F., I heard people talking about it. Maybe that is where Mr. Ramono and his family went."

"You know, I think he may be right about that, Angie," said Andrew. "It was awfully strange how quiet it was when I walked past Antonio's house. But get this straight, son, and understand that you don't have to rush over there and look for him. You have no reason to go there, and if he and his family are there, I'm sure they are being taken care of."

Andrew was closer to the truth than he realized, for at that very moment, Antonio had left his tent community to take a walk and see what was going on nearby. He had started to go crazy sitting in the tent with his children screaming and his wife continually worrying and complaining. In spite of the tragedy, the fires, and the destruction everywhere, he felt that he could not just sit still and wait around. As he approached the area of Twenty-Second and Mission, yet another fire was breaking out in an enormous three-story building that was the home of a dry goods store.

He looked at the smoke billowing and the flames roaring, as the men of the city's fire department stood there motionless for a moment. It was all just too much to take in. How could such a small squadron face this tormenting devil of a firestorm?

"Stop standing around and look for a water line, McIntyre!" shouted Dougherty. He and his men had just left the old mission, thinking that their problems were over for a short time, when this menacing monster blew up in their faces.

"All the mains are broken, as you know, Chief, but there is a cistern at Twenty-second and Shotwell. It may be enough to do the trick here sir, if we get to it in time!" replied McIntyre, with a strange mix of panic and fortitude at the same time.

"Good thinking, my man!" shouted Dougherty above the noise of the men unraveling hoses and the raging fire. "Take care of those hookups before we lose the entire city!"

"You there!" shouted McIntyre at Antonio. "Stop standing around and help me out! I need help with this hose!"

The two men worked with the unwieldy hose to run it all the way from the cistern at the Shotwell intersection to the scene where the fire was most active. It was a long way to go, but it was their only hope right now. If the water held out long enough, the plan might just work. They had the only accessible water source in the whole city, and once it ran out, that was it. The water came gushing through the hose and the firemen finally felt like they were accomplishing something. It wasn't long and the fire went out.

"Eureka!" shouted Antonio! "This is fabulous! It looks like you've finally stopped the fire from spreading!"

Indeed, most of the Mission district was spared because of the cistern. Otherwise all would have been destroyed by a fire which started with a few bad electrical wires and some coal lamps that had been overturned.

11

Enrico Caruso was considered the greatest operatic tenor of all time. Just a night ago, he had played the role of Don Jose in the musical "Carmen" and thrilled the audience with his powerful voice, his suave demeanor, and his dramatic movements on stage, but today as he heard the cries of men, women, and children after the quake, none of that seemed to matter.

Enrico's valet had come into his room shortly after the initial quake, saying, "It is nothing," but in a few short minutes, both went out into the open so the hotel wouldn't crush them to powder. The famous tenor knew it was much more than nothing, since the plaster on the ceiling had fallen like a shower, covering the bed and other furniture with a thick layer of debris. It was time to get going, so he made his way to Union Square and hoped to get on the Oakland ferry.

"You there!" he called to a man with a cart. "Take me to the Oakland ferry, and quick! I can barely breathe out here, sir!" he said to the driver as they made their way through the smoke and dust, passing terrible scenes of twisted cable car rails, burnt-out cable cars, and flaming buildings. San Francisco appeared to be disintegrating before his very eyes, and it looked like a war zone that had been bombed. Little did he know it at the time, but one by one, the city's industrial section, social hubs, and residential sections were rapidly disappearing and turning into a nightmare which no one would have dreamed possible. Homeless people were jamming the streets, and relief committees would eventually be formed to help them through the crisis. The best author in the world would have difficulty writing about the scenes flashing before him. What would be the use trying? He could only string words together and curse the futility of them.

A number of city blocks away, the famous actor John Barrymore, aged twenty-four at the time, had been sleeping off the effects of some hard drinking the night before in a hotel. He was on tour with a company of actors who was performing a Broadway hit, "The Dictator," and he had been playing the part of a telegrapher. After the show, he was celebrating with the cast the way he often did – in a state of inebriation. He was drunk during most of the earthquake, and had stumbled into the basement of the hotel. Firemen had to drag him out of it, with him putting on quite a show as he fought with them and kept complaining about them grabbing him by the shirt.

12

It had been a very long day for the Bacigalupi family and for Ned Furtado. After going to their grandparents' home in the residential district that had been unharmed by the fires, they spent that afternoon hearing Ernie's confession and taking a nap. They then had a decent, yet simple meal. They knew that they would have to make their food last for quite some time.

"Ned, we are so glad to hear that your leg was only fractured, and that they didn't have to set it," said Angelica.

"Yes, once they got me to a doctor named Charles Spencer on the other side of town, he managed to put a cast on it quick, even though there was a long line of people behind me. Luckily, I was the first one to see him today, but word got around that he was helping to care for some of the victims. If I had gotten there later, I probably would still be waiting in line outside his house like the others," said Ned.

"Well, it's a good thing you have people like Andrew and Ernie for friends," said Mrs. Furtado. "If not for them, you wouldn't be here right now, and you're all I've got, mister!"

The Furtado's home had some minor damage, but they were further away from the burned area of the city even then Andrew's extended family, and both Ned and Emily were in need of company tonight. They had no children – just the two dogs that were Skippy's parents.

There was then a knock on the door, and several neighbors had discovered that the Bacigalupi clan had survived without major damage to the house or to themselves. Many from the neighborhood had come to ask for food and blankets, and they were camped out in various parts of the home.

"It's very kind of you folks to help your neighbors out in such a time as this, but you know that these people are going to have to leave tomorrow. You simply can't feed the whole neighborhood, or you too will starve!" said Emily.

"That's true," said Ernesto Bacigalupi, Ernie's grandfather. "We'll have no choice. They'll have to go to those camps at the Presidio you were talking about, Ernie. I do hope that that is where Antonio and his family are right now."

"Well, tomorrow, we will go there and see if they have his name on the roster," said Andrew. With any luck, they will be organized to that point. We'll never find him otherwise. In the meantime, you, Ned, had better lay low and get some rest for that leg of yours. Do you have something that can help him get around, Dad?"

"We might have a cane around here somewhere. I'll check on that right away," replied Ernesto.

The next morning, after all had gotten some sleep in spite of all the noise going on in the city, Ernie and Andrew started to make their way to the Presidio and check to see if Antonio or his family was there. It was a long way to go, so they took Ernesto's horse and cart and began to try to work their way around the devastation of a burned-out city. As they rode over the twisted railway tracks of the Peninsula Railroad, they saw another wagon coming toward them with no other souls around.

"Look, Ernie! We're not seeing many other visitors today, so we'd better stop and see if this fellow knows anything about the Presidio," shouted Andrew excitedly. "Hello there, sirs! Could we trouble you for some information?"

"I'm in quite a hurry, friend, but what is it you want?" returned the man rather abruptly. The two men with him said nothing other than a very quiet hello. None of them seemed in the mood to talk.

"I'm Andrew Bacigalupi, and this is my son, Ernie." said Andrew. "Have you heard about the tent city they've put up at the Presidio? We're looking for a good friend of mine there, and hopefully they have some record of who is at this place."

"Name's Benson," the driver lied. "This is Sam and Eli – they are a couple of employees of mine. No, I haven't heard anything about it, but I do hope you find your friend. A lot of folks are looking for their friends and loved ones right now. I've got some very important business to tend to right now, if you don't mind."

With that Mr. Gianini quickly rode off toward the edge of town in the opposite direction of which Andrew and his son were headed. He had just checked his bank building and removed a large number of books and furniture. He chuckled to himself a bit at the thought that the Bacigalupis were unaware of something else in the wagon.

"Little do they know that this wagon has valuable treasure beneath a pile of oranges back there – pouches filled with $80,000 worth of silver and gold! It's a good thing I got it all out of the city just before it burned to the ground!" he said to himself.

Gianini had gone to bed feeling good about his life the day before the quake. He had wondered the next morning whether he had any bank left at all, but after making the seventeen mile trip back to San Francisco from San Mateo and seeing the catastrophe, he had other things to distract him. Some people had been shot on sight and left where they were lying. Others had been crushed under the weight of the collapsed homes or burned alive, and children were running all around the city looking for their parents. It had taken him a total of five hours to make the trip, only to see such sad sights.

When he had finally arrived at the Crocker building next door to his bank, where his money should have been kept in the vault, he was shocked to see that it was not there. Instead the bag of valuables had been left by an assistant in his own bank. He had had no choice but to make the daring decision to bring the treasure of gold and silver with him by horse and wagon back to San Mateo. He had hoped that thieves would not find him before he got there, so he was very careful about protecting his identity. If he didn't, it could cost him not only his career, but his life.

He would continue to travel under the cover of darkness all the way to San Mateo, where he secured these same pouches in the fireplace ash-trap of his second home. The fire had barely been under control in the city when he opened a temporary bank at his brother's home on Van Ness Avenue. Other large banks such as his Bank of Italy would take weeks to reopen, but he knew better than to wait that long. He knew many of his wealthiest customers on a first name basis, and it didn't take him long to help them with their accounts. With his $80,000 in gold and silver coins, he managed to cash checks for them and begin loans for rebuilding. He knew that his customers had good credit rates and loaned them money at a fair interest to help them restart their businesses. He was the one man in town who could help them rebuild their lives, and their buildings would rise from the ashes later on.

He would go on later to become one of the most respected and prestigious bankers, and his business would later grow into one of the world's banking giants – the Bank of America.

13

Ernie and Andrew continued their wagon ride to the Presidio. It was difficult to travel through or even around the part of the city where the main damage had occurred. As they rode they saw more and more destruction-more than they ever could have imagined. Men and women were wandering in the streets for safety, rather than trying to remain inside. Many of them had heard of the tent city set up at the Presidio and were headed there, sharing the information with anyone they could. Some still were unaware of such help.

"Ma'am, you should go to the Presidio right away! There is help for you and your family there!" shouted Andrew to a woman in a nightgown who was carrying a baby and walking her other child. There were men in pajamas and dinner coats, and women scantily dressed with evening wraps hastily thrown over them.

"Dad, look over there!" exclaimed Ernie, as he was pointing at another group. Sitting on a curb was an old woman grasping a bird cage, but the cage was empty. Oddly enough, the parrot that had been its resident was perched on her hand.

"Excuse me, kind sir," muttered a man carrying a pot of calla lilies. "Have you seen my Florence? I must find her... I simply must... I must... I must give her these flowers. It's her birthday, you see, and she is nowhere around. I don't know if she's alive or not! How will I find out? Where do I start to look?" he continued to mumble.

"Just go to the Presidio! All of you!" screamed Ernie as loud as he could.

"And my son! Where in the world is he?" a woman nearby called. "He was here this morning, and now he's gone. I don't know where to look for him." She was a cleaning woman with a new broom in one hand and a large hat with ostrich plumes.

"You'll find him, ma'am," said a man in an old-fashioned night shirt and swallow tails. "Don't lose hope. He could be anywhere – just keep hoping and praying that he escaped somewhere."

"Look, Dad! There are some soldiers up ahead!" said Ernie.

"Those look like troops distributing clothing and food. It looks like the government finally figured out that we have a serious emergency here! They will come in handy for maintaining order here too. Looters and crazy people start to show up during times such as these, and the people that need shelter will be taken care of in refugee camps like the tent city," returned his father.

"I guess we are pretty lucky to still be able to live with Grandma and Grandpa, huh?" said Ernie in reply. Yes, they were lucky indeed.

14

After finding their way through the deserted streets and rubble, as well as the crowds looking for shelter that marched along in sort of a daze, Ernie and Andrew finally got to the tent city at the Presidio.

"Well, that wasn't so easy, was it Ernie, with the roads being covered with debris and the streets all buckled? If it seemed like a long trip to me, it must have been even longer for you. But we will finally know what happened to Antonio. It would have been nice if he could have telegraphed us or written us, but..." trailed off Andrew.

"But desperate times call for desperate measures?" Ernie said, completing his father's sentence.

"That's right, Ernie. Nothing truer has ever been said," said Andrew emphatically.

"Well, what do we do first, Dad?"

"Take a look at your surroundings, Ernie," mentored his father.

"There is a long line over by that building over there. I'll bet that is where people are signing in," answered Ernie.

"Yes. Let's go over there... I think you struck gold. Excuse me," said Andrew after they made their way up to the long line. "Is this the sign-in line?"

"No sir," said the ragged looking woman. "This is the line to check in loved ones. The sign-in is at the other side of this building, and it's a long one!"

"Longer even than this one, eh?" asked Ernie.

"Yes, son, I guess so, but lucky for us we need to be in this shorter line, and we are already in the right place by happenstance," replied Andrew.

After waiting about thirty minutes, Andrew and Ernie got to the list which was on a cloth-covered, make-shift table. They were afraid to ask after all that anticipation, but ask Andrew did.

"We are wanting to know if Antonio Ferrante and his family made it here to the tent city. We can't find any trace of them anywhere else, so we were hoping that they made it here."

"Let's see," said the attendant. " Ferrante.... Ferrante... he muttered to himself. "Ah! Here it is, Antonio Ferrante, his wife Maria, a son, and a daughter. That should be all of them."

"Yes, my good man, it is!" said Andrew with joy. "It must be that they all escaped from the house before it collapsed and then just wandered around until they got help."

"Well, that was true for a lot of these folks!" said the weary attendant. "Now you'll have to move along because the line is long."

"But how can we find him?" asked Ernie.

"Your guess is as good as mine, friend," replied the attendant. "We have all we can do to just keep people from dying of starvation and heat exhaustion right now."

After searching for quite some time through camp one, Andrew and Ernie finally found the Ferrantes. They looked much worse than they last remembered them. Their faces were withered from the heat and blackened from searching for their belongings through the rubble that was once their home. After hugging one another and thanking God aloud for sparing them all, Antonio began to speak of what had happened prior to coming to the Presidio.

"Here we are on the prairie, just like the pioneers before us," said Antonio. "I guess we can be thankful that we are still alive."

"As are we," said Andrew.

"The barbarians around us are not safe!" said Antonio's wife, Maria. "Just this morning, some tried to invade our tent looking for food! They just charged in here, drunk on whiskey that they got from the militiamen, and started rummaging through what little things we had left. I had managed to find a little bit of bread and water from the ice chest in the rubble, but now they have even taken that. There is no food anywhere!"

As they were speaking, embers hovering over the tents threatened to set them ablaze at any moment.

"We've been very busy just keeping our tent from going up in flames," said Antonio. "The fires in the city are not that far away, and the air is filled with these little matchsticks! When we are not putting out the fire on our own tent, we are helping others to do it. I met a teenager named Jimmy Ho just a while ago who said that he was ready to die. He had three choices, he said. One was to simply wait to burn to death. Another was to starve to death. The third was to drown himself. As he started running toward the water, he said that he planned to join his ancestors. That is just one of the many tragedies that we have seen firsthand here, Andy."

"We ran to stop him, but he overpowered us," said Maria. "When we got back to our tent, the children told us that we had been robbed. What few things I could salvage from the house are now all gone! My wedding picture, my jewelry chest, my mother's locket...." she continued, sobbing quietly.

"Some bad men came by after that!" said Richard, their youngest child. "They started shooting the men as they were running away!"

"Yes, it's true," said their father. "The military men here seem no better than anyone. It seems that once they become soldiers, they don't have to use their brains anymore. In times like these, they think they are gods or something, and that they can do whatever they please. They even tell women to give shots of whiskey to their babies to make them calm down or put them in a drunken state. These men are horrid, Andrew."

"Well, I suppose that in a sense they are following orders," said Antonio, snuffing out some more embers on the tent. "The higher ups have probably given them ultimate authority to shoot to kill, whether they think people are scavenging for their own things or looting. I'm sure it's hard to tell which of those things is really going on. Everybody looks alike, with their same suits and hats. It's just one of the tragedies of an event like this. People all go crazy and get desperate. Some are just looking for food, others are looking to steal. As we were riding over here in the wagon, we saw many people trying to charge ridiculous prices for what little food and valuables are left. It's a crime to do such a thing when people are hurting and dying. Just a crime! The Chinese people here are afraid to come out of their tents. After forty years of persecution, they think that the guns of the fortress here are going to be turned on them."

"I heard that it's the same way in Golden Gate Park," said Andrew. "People are living in tents, but they have no food or water, and they are going to die without it. We managed to get a little bit of water from a fireman who used his steam engine to make it. Have you been able to get water?"

"Precious little!" said Maria. "The soldiers are getting a little bit of it from somewhere, but there is not enough to go around. Lord knows what will become of the baby that was born here just a few tents down from us. There was quite a bit of commotion when that happened, what with the mother screaming and all. Antonio took the children for a walk so they wouldn't have to hear it."

"What a time to have to bear a child!" said Antonio. "When all the food supply stores have burned down and there is no water to be had. We've seen loved ones carrying tin cans from the ruins and filling them at the gutters where the fire engines made a stream. That is how we got what little we had, but what do we do now? Try to boil some seawater? It's just not that easy!"

Just then another refugee walked up to their tent.

"I'm a banker," said the man. "I'll give you ten dollars for a piece of that bread your little girl is eating."

"But mister," said Maria's little girl, Annie. "This is all we have, and then all our food is gone."

"Don't you worry about it, missy," said the banker. "I forgot. My bank burned down to the ground, and I don't think I have money left in my wallet anyway." He then turned and walked away.

By that point everyone, including Andrew, Ernie, and the Ferrantes, was exhausted. They all drifted to sleep on the chilly slope of the sandy dune that was their current dwelling at the Presidio. Sleep came in small doses, and it was mercifully doled out to them by the hand of God for a short time. The fires burned continuously and created a red glow that nearly extinguished the sunlight. There was no regular sense of time anymore. During catastrophic events, one thinks in terms of hours rather than days, and the days just blend together without thought for regular schedules or routines.

15

The Ferrantes and the Bacigulupis were awakened early the next morning by explosions in the city that seemed much too close for comfort.

"Excuse me, sir," said a middle-aged woman who had approached their tent. "My name is Jessie, and this is my mother. She is old and so tired that she can no longer walk. We have already walked all over the city and we just can't walk anymore. Our house is gone, like many others, gone to the flames. A friend let us stay in his apartment, but then the dynamiting started and we had to leave there too. We just don't know what to do anymore."

"Ma'am, I'm so sorry to hear that," said Antonio. "All you can do for now is try to get a tent and stay here. It is safer than going to the city. Then hopefully we will get some food and water."

The woman then stumbled off with her ancient mother into the dawn and in search of a tent, with the eerie glow of the burning buildings silhouetting their slouching figures.

"I truly wish we could help them all," said Andrew.

"Me too," replied Antonio. "I suppose we just did help in a minor fashion – the best we could. We can barely help ourselves, much less them."

"Well, Antonio, you must not lose hope either," said Andrew. "For now, you and your family are at least out of harm's way, and relief from outside sources may soon come. It just seems bad right now, my friend. Ernie and I are going to take the southern route back home to Angelica's parents' home in the Western Addition. If there is any food and water left, we will bring some for you and your little ones as soon as we can, but I don't think it is wise for you to bring them over there quite yet. For all we know, the fires may have spread to that part of town too. They were very close when we left."

"You're a wise man, Andy," said Maria. "We are all too weak to go on foot, so if you can come back later with a bigger wagon to get us, that would be wonderful. In the meantime, God be with you, and be careful – especially of the soldiers. They are doing more harm than good sometimes."

And so Andrew and Ernie began their journey back toward home. Little did they know the troubles that awaited them just a few miles ahead. As they rumbled over cobblestone streets in their small cart and the horse pulled them faithfully along, they were appalled by what they saw. The park was a huge area of several hundred acres, and it had been the brainchild of John McClaren, a well-known engineer. He had changed it from a cluster of sand dunes into a beautifully decorated set of gardens, filled with cypress and eucalyptus trees. It had been a place where children played joyfully on merry-go-rounds or traveled in goat-pulled carts through many winding pathways. Those romantically inclined would take boat rides on Stow Lake and stroll through the Japanese gardens.

But today was a different experience from all that. It was now swarming with thousands and thousands of people who were very desperate to help their families and children survive. Some were lying face down in the grass, as if dead, while others didn't seem to be able to grasp the fact that their loved ones were gone.

"Look Dad," said Ernie quietly as they rode past a woman holding a baby. The baby was not moving, and was obviously dead, but the woman continued to coo and caress her as if she were alive.

"Hey mister," shouted a young girl sitting near a tree, stroking the hair of her doll. "Do you like my doll? I rescued her from the fire! She's safe now!" She was sitting with a group of other children who had been orphaned during the fires. They were now being watched by a small group of nuns.

"Dad, these people seem crazy!" said Ernie.

"You would be crazy too if you had been through what they have," said his father calmly. "Many of these people are not going to make it, because drugs and treatment centers are scarce. Who knows how many hospitals are even left? If they aren't part of the burned area, they are still hard to get to, and some of these people just don't have that much time left. Without food or water, they'll die. For sure without water they will.

"Then give them some of ours, Dad!" replied Ernie.

"We'll have to do it carefully, since our supply is very limited too and we may be swarmed upon by a crowd. Wait for the right time, Son, and maybe we can help a few," said Andrew.

As they rode on, they were soon approached by a young man with a wife and baby. They were out of sight for a brief moment from the crowds, and this family was very deserving of help.

"Hello," said the young husband. "Do you have any water? Our baby will die soon without it, and my wife can't go on much longer either."

"Of course," said Andrew. "But please spare us some as well because I have a wife and family too."

The man handed the tin can to his wife, who drank some and then gave some to her baby. The mother would need the water to be able to nurse the child.

"Thank you so much!" said the woman. "God bless you!"

"We're glad to help!" said Ernie as they rode on. "Dad, when do you think they'll get outside help? Where is everybody?" he asked with a sense of shock and bewilderment.

"Son, there is just no way to get them to refugee centers right now. Whatever horses and vehicles are available, most of the transportation and manpower is going toward putting out the fires. All we can do is hope that they put them out soon," said Andrew wearily.

"What was that?" shouted Ernie. "I think I heard a gunshot, Dad!"

"It sounds like it came from over there by that big eucalyptus tree," said Andrew quietly. He could see that there were a number of male refugees being gathered together into a huddle, and it looked like there was a militia man standing near them with his gun in the air. As they got a little closer, they could hear him giving the men orders.

"Now who is in charge of this little playground, here, eh?" said the sergeant, who was somewhat intoxicated from too much whiskey.

A man named Bush stood forward.

"Name is Bush, sir, and I am the superintendent of the playground." What that really meant was that he often did babysitting for the children there. They trusted him and loved him, as he was a kind man. "I left my burned-out home to come and be with them, since I heard about the crowds here and how frightened they would be."

"Well, they'll be happy to know that food and water has finally arrived. We just need them to help carry the provisions to the hungry. Get some volunteers to carry these cartons, and hurry!" shouted the sergeant.

"But these people are too exhausted to carry those heavy cartons! They've lost all their meager possessions, they've just narrowly escaped with their lives, and are weak and hungry," replied the superintendent. "I can hire a driver with a wagon so that people don't have to carry the cartons."

"Keep out of this!" the military man snarled. "Just who is giving the orders here? Now shut up and get out of here, before I do something I may regret."

"But Sergeant, you know who I am! I'm just trying to help and encourage these people. I mean you no disrespect," replied the man.

"No, I don't know you, and I don't want to know you!" answered the sergeant angrily.

Ernie and Andrew continued to watch this drama from a slight distance, but they could hear every word of the conversation. Suddenly, as the superintendent began to walk away, the sergeant drew his revolver and shot him twice in the back.

"Is there anyone else in this group that questions my authority?" asked the drunken sergeant. With that, the men quickly began unloading the cartons and distributing them to those nearby.

"Dad, we've got to tell someone what happened!" said Ernie. "He should not get away with that!"

"We'll do what we can about it, but I'm afraid it will have to wait, Ernie, until the fires are all put out and things start to get more back to normal. For now, we've got to focus on getting back home and helping Antonio and his family however we can. At least for now they have food."

"You there! You and the boy! Get down from that wagon and help out! The name's Harrington, and I'm in charge here! We need that wagon to help distribute this food and water, and when we're done with that, there is a lot of cleanup to do. If you think you're riding out of here, think again," said the sergeant. "What are your names?"

"The name's Andrew Bacigalupi, and this is my son."

"Well, boys, there is a lot of work to be done, so join the other men and get moving!"

Rather than argue with the murderous sergeant, Andrew and Ernie both knew they had better cooperate. They had seen first-hand what happened to those who spoke at all.

"It looks like our plans have changed, huh, Dad?" said Ernie.

"They sure have, son, but I have an idea. After this is all through, we can probably bring some of this food and water back to Antonio and his family. It's not that far to return there soon, but we have to be careful about things. We don't want Harrington to know that we have kept one of these cartons, so we'll have to figure out how to hide it and rescue them later."

"Well, what are you two waiting for? Get that cart of yours over here and start loading up," said Harrington.

"Yes, sir!" said Andrew.

The cart was quickly loaded with about 20 cartons, and that was about all the small vehicle could hold. Ernie and Andrew quickly distributed the cartons to various areas of the park, while the other men opened them up and passed out the supplies. The food and water brought optimism to the people, and they know longer had blank stares on their faces, but a new attitude, one of hope and thankfulness for some much needed relief from the city officials in charge.

"I knew that things would start to look better, Dad!" said Ernie, as he munched on an apple from the carton.

The army had ordered that all grocers give away their goods for free to stop businesses from selling them at ridiculous prices, and even the army officials provided food from their storehouses at the Presidio. Considering how close the Presidio was to Golden Gate Park, it was surprising that it took as long as it did to get there, but the wheels of progress sometimes turn slowly during hard times.

Despite such efforts by kind and helpful officials, there was still an atmosphere of fear and intimidation because of the attitudes of the men in uniform. Some of them took their responsibility seriously, while others claimed privileges that were only used during martial law. Such martial law had never actually been proclaimed, though most people thought it had. Many of the young soldiers were both frightened and cruel to the crowds, forcing them to move with the point of a bayonet, and sometimes using it. Because the city was being controlled by such amateurs, who were not really trained in their jobs, clashes with authority were frequent and unnecessarily dangerous. The army was handling everything west of Van Ness Avenue, including Golden Gate Park and the army post, where most of the refugees were congregating, while the militia and police were in charge of the severely scorched eastern section.

As Andrew and Ernie finished up the last of their first load, Ernie noticed something odd.

"Dad, did you see all those cases of liquor that the sergeant and his men were opening?" he asked.

"Yes, son, I did," answered Andrew. "I'm sure they were ordered to destroy all the liquor stocks, but they just couldn't bring themselves to throw it down into the sewer when they could pour it down their throats instead. "

"Well, it sure is making things worse, with them drinking so much. I can smell it all over them, and it is making them do stupid things. Who knows who they will shoot next?" asked Ernie.

"Just do what you are told, Ern, and hopefully we will get out of this mess soon," said his father.

And so the day continued, with Ernie and Andrew bringing load after load of supplies to various parts of the park. They went all the way around Stow Lake and even further, seeing many people close to the point of death being revived once again. Though it was all very rewarding to be helping in this way, it wasn't easy because the crowds would often get out of control and push and shove to get the food. Even some of the children were getting trampled in the process, but most were spared from injury by some decent person nearby who pulled them out of harm's way just in time.

As Ernie and Andrew pulled up to the sergeant and his men, they couldn't help but notice that their drinking had gotten much more excessive. Things just seemed to be going from bad to worse.

"You wouldn't believe what happened over by the south side of Stow Lake," said one of the drunks – an army man who could barely stand up any more. "I started giving out food and some idiot grabbed it right out of my hands! I couldn't just let people keep doing that, so I gave him a stab in the leg with my bayonet. Well, you can bet it wasn't a problem after that, can't you boys?"

The others just laughed and laughed at the thought of it all. They were acting like drunken sailors rather than men of the law, and it was a despicable thing to behold.

"Okay, Ern, I think this is our chance!" said Andrew. "We've got one case left in the cart, and they are so drunk that they won't even notice us leaving."

"Are you sure, Dad?" said Ernie.

"Yes, as sure as I can be right now."

The two of them slowly headed for the horse drawn cart, dodging behind cypress trees when they could and trying to be as inconspicuous as possible, though it was broad daylight now. They crept up to the cart and pulled on the reins.

"Hey! Where are those two going?" said the drunken Harrington with a pitiful slurred tongue. "Get over here now, you fools!"

The shots that rang through the air brought a chill to Andrew's spine. It had just missed Ernie by a few feet, but Andrew was shot in the arm. They both took off as fast as the horse could go, with Harrington and his men running after them, but the men were so intoxicated that they just stumbled around when trying to run. They quickly gave up the chase and returned to their business. They had more whiskey to get rid of.

"Hey Dad! That was close! Are you all right?"

"I'll be okay, son. Just tear off my shirt sleeve so I can use it as a tourniquet.

"We have to get you to a doctor, Dad!"

"In due time, son. Let's just get this stuff to Antonio before those men sober up," said Andrew. "Maybe he or someone at the Presidio can help me with this bullet."

"But you're bleeding, Dad!"

"That's what the tourniquet is for. Now just tie that nice and tight for me, and I'll be alright."

As they got nearer to the Presidio's refugee camp, Andrew started to feel much worse. Losing blood was the last thing he needed right now, when he was already exhausted and tired after passing out cartons of supplies. Ernie took over driving for him halfway there, and when they pulled up to the receiving area for refugees, they were greeted by a friendly face. Not only was it friendly, but it was also military. Evidently there were still a few good men left, and the officer quickly introduced himself and brought Andrew and Ernie to a nurse for attention to the wound.

"Officer O'Malley, the man who did this to me was named Harrington," said Andrew. "He nearly killed me and my son as we were leaving the compound at the park. He was trying to shoot us in the back, just like he did to some other poor soul there who was trying to give him some advice."

"We'll see to it that he answers to a higher authority, Mr. Bacigalupi," said O'Malley. Deep down, O'Malley knew that it would be hard to prosecute Harrington, considering the current attitude and mismanagement that existed among his superiors – that of disorder and a sense of entitlement to do whatever they darned well pleased during extraordinary circumstances.

"Glad to hear it, sir," answered Andrew weakly.

The nurses removed the bullet after giving Andrew some of the whiskey that was so plentiful at the Presidio. As it burned its way down his throat and numbed his senses, he was indeed grateful for the anesthetic, and was quickly stitched up and sent on his way with a bottle of water and some bread.

Ernie was waiting right beside him through the whole process, and he helped him get back in the cart so they could head over to Antonio and his family once again.

"Ernie!" shouted Antonio, as he saw the horse and cart pulling up. "Are you a sight for sore eyes! Andrew, my God, what happened to you?" he asked after seeing the bandages on his arm.

"Just a flesh wound!" said Andrew. "Some crazy men tried to kill us, but we got away. Here is some food and water for you all! Drink it now! You've been waiting long enough for better stuff than they've been giving you here. Have they given anything at all?"

"Just small amounts of water and cold pork and beans," said Antonio. "But this will definitely help! Thank you so much, my friends."

"Antonio, we can't just leave you here like this. You must come and stay with us - you and your family. We'll take turns riding in the cart, but we'll get there eventually, even if some of us have to walk," said Andrew.

"Yes, you've got to come!" Ernie chimed in.

"That is very kind of you both," said Antonio. "We will join you, even if the journey is difficult. We can't take much more of this insanity here. It is too hard for us all."

"Very well, then," said Andrew. "Pack up what few things you have, and let's be off. I can still see the fires on the east side, but we will stay to the west and try to steer clear of Harrington and his men. They are the ones who shot us while we were trying to get away from them. It's a long story, and I'll tell you all about it on the way home."

16

Thus began the journey back to the Western Addition, where Ernie's family was eagerly awaiting news of what had happened over the last day. Could it really have been only twenty-four or a few more hours since this nightmare began? When would it all end? Would they make it safely past Golden Gate Park, and once they got past it, would the home of his grandparents still be there? The Ham and Eggs fire was dangerously close by – a little too close by for their liking, and it could easily have spread to his grandparents' home by now. If only there was some way to communicate, but all communication lines were down right now. There was very little communication for miles around, so the only way to find anything out was through rumors or by going somewhere in person.

As they approached Golden Gate Park once again, everyone kept an eye out for the army men. Instead of guardians of the people, they had become wicked soldiers of the gun and bayonet. They were always afraid of what they would see next, since these men had a self-proclaimed license to kill, and they were not afraid to use it. By going around the northern perimeter of the park, Andrew and his passengers managed to avoid confronting them. It took great patience to do so, however, since the roads were so bad and there was mass confusion everywhere.

"Dad, do you know where we are?" asked Ernie, as they rode the cart over the rough cobblestone roads. This was not the severe burn district, but it was still quite disorienting to try to find their way around, with it getting dark once again and the fires of the city continually creating a haze everywhere. There was a blanket of smoke that had covered the entire peninsula, and it was disconcerting to say the least.

"Well, Ernie, we were smart to stay out of Golden Gate Park. It would have been out of our way to go further into it. All we can hope for now is to get back to your grandparents soon and see if they are alright, as well as your mother and Esther. I'm a little worried about them," said Andrew.

"Yeah - me too, Dad. It just is hard not knowing anything. Hopefully they were able to hold back the fires," replied Ernie.

"It looks to me like we are somewhere near Hayes Street," said his father. "If we can stay on Hayes we can keep going east to Gough and then head north to your grandparents' house. It shouldn't take that long once we get to Gough."

The way things turned out, it was a mistake to try to make it to Gough Street and Hayes. This just happened to be in the outer edge of the burned out district. When they were within a block of Gough Street, they noticed a handful of men with shovels, picking up debris in the street. There was a militia man from the east side of town in charge of forcing innocent bystanders to clean up messes. Unfortunately, these militia men were often more cruel and unscrupulous than the soldiers from the Presidio, but Andrew had no way of knowing this.

As Andrew and his young son drove past the group, they were immediately stopped by the militia man.

"You there! Get down immediately, you and the boy! We need help here and there's not enough manpower to go around. The name's Sheelin. By the authority given to me by the mayor of this city, I order you to help these men with their shoveling. As a leader of this amateur safety committee, I have my orders."

"But sir, I really need to get back to my wife and family," said Andrew." They could be in grave danger, and I haven't seen them for over twenty-four hours. My son and I are exhausted from helping the soldiers at Golden Gate Park and supplying food to the people there. We nearly escaped with our lives after a drunken soldier shot at us both."

"You must have been doing something wrong," said the man. "Did you try to take things into your own hands? The only people being shot are looters, and we've had to shoot quite a few of those. Those filthy scoundrels deserved it too – taking advantage of the situation like they did. We have orders to kill more if it keeps up."

"No, sir, we did nothing wrong. We were only trying to help," said Ernie with a tremble in his voice.

"Sir, I will ask you once and once only that you silence your boy," replied Sheelin. I haven't got time to deal with children right now. Your city needs you and that's all there is to it. Now start shoveling, or I'll shoot!"

Rather than get mixed up in another shooting incident, Andrew and Ernie hastily grabbed shovels and started working with the other men.

"You better do as he says," said one older man in a black suit. "Sheelin just shot about fifty men, with the help of other men like him. They were rounded up and shot firing-squad style. Don't question him or talk back to him, whatever you do. There is no telling what might happen to you or to all of us for that matter.

As they continued shoveling pieces of cement and lumber into the wagon, Ernie and his father tried to be as quiet as possible. For all they knew they could be doing this for days, and they needed to get back as soon as possible. Making a run for it like they did before was just too risky.

After about an hour, Andrew finally broke the silence once he saw that Sheelin was a good distance away from them all. He began to quietly ask the men nearby what they had done to deserve being arrested and forced to work as if they were criminals.

"I guess you could say I really was looting," said a younger man whose face was brown and sweaty, "if you want to call searching for food looting. It was either that, or my family would starve. My wife is pregnant, and she needs food and water desperately. As I was foraging through some rubble, Sheelin grabbed me and started questioning me. I could smell whiskey on his breath, and I actually saw him steal it through a broken window of a shop. He is no better than anyone else in this town. We're all just trying to survive."

"How long has it been since you saw your wife?" questioned Andrew.

"Ever since this holocaust began," said the man. "I simply stepped out of my house to search for food when I was forced to do what we are doing right now."

"I was given permission by a store owner," said another weary older man. "I shopped at his store every day, and we knew each other on a first name basis. He felt sorry for me and for many others, and he was kind enough to help out rather than try to gouge us on prices when we have nothing! But these "amateurs" are truly what they say they are. They are not police or soldiers, just ordinary citizens taking the law into their own hands, playing judge and jury!"

"So you want me to play judge and jury?" shouted Sheelin from behind. He suddenly appeared out of nowhere and had obviously heard everything the older man said.

In Sheelin's mind there was no time for questioning or for trials. He shot the poor man before he could say any more.

"Any more liars want to complain about me or my actions? Step forward and join the others who have had the nerve to do it! You will meet your Maker faster than you planned, just like the rest of these crooks!"

Ernie began to cry – to cry harder than he ever had before. He had never witnessed a murder this close up. Andrew held him close and told him to stay quiet as possible. The nightmare of the fires and the earthquake, as well as the images of the starving people they had helped... it all paled in significance to what they were now witnessing. It was as if hell had unleashed demons that were were taking over the souls of men who had been ordinary citizens just a day before. When would it all end, and would things ever be the same again? Most likely they never would be - surely not for Ernie.

Sheelin pulled his victim aside and ordered the men to do the unthinkable.

"Bury him! Bury him now, all of you, before we have to dig more graves!" he shouted maniacally.

Two of the men near Sheelin immediately dropped what they were doing and started digging a shallow grave in a nearby grassy area. Tears were streaming down their faces as they did so, fearing that they might be next.

So the shoveling continued, as the flames of the nearby city burned as if propelled by propane. Why couldn't more be done to save this magnificent city? Smoke was choking the men as they shoveled, and just when they thought they couldn't stand any more of the abuse and intimidation, hope came in the form of a messenger from Sheelin's commanders.

"Sir, you are desperately needed on Mission Avenue," said the messenger. " The lawlessness is out of control there, and these men have paid the due penalty for their crimes. Let them go and head immediately to Mission and Market. You will receive further orders upon your arrival."

"Well, what do you know, boys?" said Sheelin to his men. "It looks like you're getting off easy today, but I'll be back here tomorrow, so if you're smart, you'll see the error of your ways and start doing some good in this town. Now get out of my sight, all of you, and don't let me catch you stealing anymore, or you'll get a sign put over your dead bodies, telling the whole world that you are looters instead of people who care about their neighbors during hard times like these."

It was indeed hard to take such criticism from a murderer such as Sheelin. He didn't take time to ask questions or believe anyone who spoke the truth, and he himself had been guilty of stealing whiskey from various locations. His father had been a forty-niner who could put away his liquor better than most, and it seemed to Andrew as if he was reliving those crazy and insane times. It was as if the clock went backward in many respects. Instead of a thriving city, there was now a war zone that looked like it had been bombed by a large army. Instead of the clatter of horse hooves in the streets and the din of newsboys shouting everywhere, there was emptiness and a strange quiet in many areas.

As Andrew drove the little horse-led cart to Franklin and O'Farrell, he couldn't help but notice poor Ernie, asleep from exhaustion and lying beside him in a childlike fashion. Though he had become a man in many respects, he was still also a boy who had witnessed things that boys should never see.

It was now quite late in the evening, the second day of the fires, and they were in no way appearing to stop. As one part of the city would finally burn itself out, another would seem to burst into flames, despite all the dynamite being used to stop the spreading. Instead of slowing it down, it was actually creating more oxygen and wind to spread the fires even further. Instead of valiant firefighters putting the flames out with water, they had to simply watch them burn.

Such was the case to the south of Ernie's grandparents, the Bartons. As they approached the home, they couldn't believe that it was still standing. The fires had come so close to the home that it was beyond comprehension how it was spared, but the hand of God had done so and Andrew prayed a silent prayer of thanks. It seemed that the immediate threat was over for now, and that the wind was now blowing in its natural eastward fashion, which was the answer to why it had been spared. Just a small shift westward would have created a whole different set of circumstances, and Andrew hated to think what could have happened if that were the case.

"Son, wake up!" said Andrew. "We are almost there! Everything looks like it is okay. If your grandpa was smart, he stayed in the house."

As the cart wobbled over the cobblestone street, Ernie looked at the home of his grandparents once again. It took on an entirely different meaning to him now. He could see Esther's face peeking through the window. She spotted them as soon as they were within range and came running out of the house in her nightgown.

"Daddy, Daddy! You're back, and Ernie is too!" she shouted with joy. "Where have you been all this time? We were so worried about you when you didn't come back! I'll go tell Mommy right away!"

Andrew and Ernie didn't wait for the others to come back. They both ran in the house as fast as they could and hugged and squeezed everyone in the family. They had all been spared so far, and that was quite a thing to be thankful for considering what they had just been through.

"Andy! We were expecting the worst, when you didn't come back, but our prayers were answered!" said Angelica, weeping and smiling at the same time.

That night, all of the adults stood by the windows watch over the flaming city, just a few blocks away from them. Everyone in the Banicalupi family was worn out and tired to the point that they had to be shaken to be awakened for their duty call. All the time, Ernie was wondering if the wind would shift, or if the natural firebreaks of wide boulevards like Van Ness would fail to do their job, but everything stayed constant for the time being. He wasn't sure what the next day held in store for him, but he knew he needed to get his strength back before he could do anything.

17

There was no rest for the firemen who were risking their lives continuously to rescue those still in the burning city. John Dougherty was one of those men. Throughout the conflagration, he had been driving his buggy from one fire line to the next, managing to keep in check many of the earlier fires, rooftop blazes, and chimneys that had crumbled and started other fires. The flames were now eating away at each other and stretching out in every possible direction of the eastern side of San Francisco.

The firestorm was going in circles as if at the hand of some merciless demon that was playing with it. Temperatures were reaching as high as 2,000 degrees Fahrenheit, and the heat was so intense that buildings over a hundred feet away would instantaneously combust from it. Libraries and museums that contained priceless books, portraits by famous artists, and documents that had held up for centuries were gone in a matter of hours, never to be seen again.

The wind was so powerful that within an hour Rincon Hill south of Market became a monster of a blaze, pouring ash and smoke into the sky and lighting up the waterfront area. It was at that moment in time that a Navy Lieutenant named Fredrick Freeman arrived in San Francisco on his Bainbridge Class destroyer, the USS Preble. The ship could not have shown up at a more opportune moment.

"We can use the fireboat and the tug to pump sea water up the hill!" he shouted to his men. The crew worked feverishly to carry out the procedure and begin the daunting task of saving what it could of San Francisco.

"Yes, sir!" the men shouted as they pumped. All hands on deck were helping in the operation.

"Move that hose, men! We haven't got much time!" shouted Freeman.

As they worked, other firemen were stamping out smoldering embers with wet blankets, or they were busy throwing the wet blankets from the gutters over the heads of the firemen holding the hose. Two would hold the hose and two others would keep them from burning alive by using the wet blankets. Every few minutes, when the men could not stand the intense heat, they would roll in the gutters, only to dry off within a few minutes again. Caps were burned and baked on their heads. Their feet were blistered by the heat inside their rubber boots. Doctors and nurses were standing by to give them strychnine in order to keep up their work. All the men were getting delirious, and whenever they received a break, they would appear indifferent to the whole scene, as if watching a silent movie. Some firemen had even done some looting themselves - they took food for their breakfast from a grocery store and washed it down with beer, attempting to achieve some sense of normalcy in the midst of chaos.

But the fire had gotten too much out of control. Old men and women were being carried from their homes by cots, and firemen took turns carrying them.

"Shoot the water over their heads!" cried one fireman, who was surrounded by flames himself.

"Help! I'm on fire!" cried the young man a moment later. Within seconds his comrades had managed to put out his uniform with their hoses, but he had third degree burns on his arms and hands and was writhing in pain.

"Quick, wrap him up with those wet blankets and bring him some first-aid!" shouted Freeman.

"We have to get these horses and this engine up the hill if we are going to be able to keep up with this monster at all!"

shouted Freeman. "See if you can get some of those people in the crowd over there to help!"

About five hundred people were rounded up and they began pulling the engine, with its team of horses, up the enormous hill, in order to keep the fire from spreading further still.

The fire was now pouring up the hill at such an incredible rate that any plan of escape for those left behind was impossible. Many died before help or aid could get to them, and Freeman's men could only do so much to help in their rescue since they were so busy trying to hold off the flames and save the ones they could. People were screaming and running in all directions, and panic about loved ones took over and created additional mayhem in the streets.

By 2:20 P.M. an operator at the telegraph office urgently reported the damage nearby his building at Market and Montgomery, stating that the Call Building, the magnificent City Hall Dome, St. Ignatius Church and College, the Old Flood Building, and the entire Examiner building had fallen to the ground in a heap. In addition, he reported that the buildings that were left were being dynamited to create firebreaks. When he at last signed off he ran as fast as he could to escape.

To make matters even worse, there were some turning to desperate measures to collect fire insurance on their homes. Seeing that some of their homes had been damaged by the earthquake but not burned down, they became arsonists to collect the fire insurance. The evil entity causing people to do things they wouldn't normally dream of doing was at work once again, and the city was now doomed to be completely devastated by fire. If the damage would have stopped after the earthquake the task would not have been as monumental, but that proved to be impossible due to a combination of many factors all working against it – the lack of preparedness by the fire department, the corruption and greed in city hall, the ineffective water mains, the weak system of gas lines, telephone lines, and building structures – all played a role in the destruction.

Although Freeman had thought his plan was not going to work out and that the city would still go up in flames, he continued his efforts to run his mile-long hose across Telegraph Hill and up Broadway toward the Montgomery Block.

"Three cheers for old Freeman!" shouted the other firemen who had been fighting so valiantly with John Dougherty. "He did it! Now that's some water pressure!"

They poured water incessantly on the entire block with the powerful pumps from Freeman's craft and were able to save many of the warehouses full of whiskey. They stood like forts in the middle of a fire-ravaged zone of the city. In the middle of the firefight, a representative of the Hoteling Whiskey Company even stopped by the exhausted firemen who had time to take a rest to thank them and lift their spirits.

"Boys," said the company representative. "Due to your courage and willingness to put yourself in harm's way, the Hoteling Whiskey Company wishes to show our thanks to you for keeping our establishment safe. Here are some cans of tomatoes that should wet your throats and make you feel better."

"Hey, these are some great tomatoes!" said Freeman, downing some fiery brown liquid from the tomato can.

"Can I have some tomatoes, boss?" laughed Dougherty, who was obviously quite thirsty himself.

"They'll calm your nerves, these tomatoes," said Freeman.

"Indeed they will, boss! Come on men, "tomatoes" for everybody.

Rather than eat tomatoes, the men downed the liquor as fast as they could. It turned out to be just what they needed after facing the devastation of the fires and the trauma of it all.

By Friday at midnight, firemen were again busy fighting the flames on the wharf at Kearny street. They now had backup from the state fireboat Governor Irwin as well as other navy ships.

"Where are all the police?" asked Freeman of his fellow officers.

Freeman could not believe how things had disintegrated within the police department. Here at the most critical point of the fire, where buildings could still be saved on the waterfront, the fire department and the Navy were fighting their own battle without the help of the city. Sweat was pouring from his brow as he took complete control of the entire waterfront district. His wrinkled, blackened face was that of a true leader of men.

"Come on men, give it all you got!" Freeman shouted, fully aware that they were about to collapse from hysteria and malnutrition as well as a lack of fresh water.

"Purgatory! That's what this is!" screamed Dougherty.

"This hard-driving wind isn't making matters any better!" returned Freeman. "We'll just have to sock it to 'em, wind or no wind!"

Meanwhile, cabin steward Sing Hoy was the highest ranking man still on board. With all the rest of the men manning the hoses, he had assumed full command of the Governor Irwin.

"Is there anyone else left on ship?" asked Dougherty.

"Thank God we have Sing at the wheel!" answered Freeman. "He may be a Chinese cook, but he's a good man!"

Sing's promotion said a lot about Freeman and his men. Not only were they courageous firemen, but they could also put their prejudices aside in times like these and look at the good inside people.

Thanks to the help of the Navy and the San Francisco Fire Department, the Ferry building as well as the Montgomery Block and other buildings on the waterfront were among the only survivors of the great conflagration.

By Friday, the fires had been burning a full three days. Five-hundred-eight city blocks, or four-point-seven square miles were annihilated by the flames primarily. The fires had traveled north toward Russian and Telegraph Hills, and San Franciscans had been holding their ground only to see most of the territory around these areas consumed.

The wooden docks which were used to bring supplies in and out of the city survived these three days of continuous fire only to go up in blazes by Friday. With the help of firefighters and fireboats, only a portion of the docks was destroyed. By Saturday at 7:15 a.m., the fires hissed and finally came to a halt. Very few buildings near the docks survived the fire except the Ferry Building and the warehouses nearby it which were built in the late 1870s.

18

As the men on the waterfront were wrapping up their firefighting endeavors, there were others sleeping in their own beds not far away that Saturday morning.

A loud knock came on the Barton home, where Andrew Bacigalupi and his family had sought safety during the turmoil of the last couple of days. Living right on the edge of the disaster area was a very trying thing for those who had been spared from the fire. What would happen next was continually on their minds and whatever rest they could find was usually interrupted quickly.

Self-preservation had been their goal during this brief period of time, but it looked like that was all about to end. "Open up, right away!" shouted the policeman. "The fire is over, and we need all able-bodied men to help with debris removal and other matters!"

Andrew opened the door and stood before the man calmly and well-rested after having slept more than 24 hours. He and his family had needed the rest, though it was often fitful due to the noise and commotion constantly going on right next to them.

"I'd be glad to help, officer. Is there any news of further provisions yet for the refugees and the rest of us? Has Washington stepped in yet?"

"Yes, thanks to Secretary of War Taft and President Roosevelt, there is talk of relief coming soon," answered the man. "We will help you get whatever you need, but right now it is urgent that you and anyone else in your family who is able help us look for anyone who may still be surviving or who are dead. Many family members are waiting for notification, and no one is sitting in their home when his fellow man needs him so desperately!"

Andrew knew that the policeman was right. Both he and Ernie could now help once again after getting some sleep and food. They simply could not rest while so many were suffering and dying.

"Very well, then. Meet us at 8:00 at O'Farrell and Franklin," said the policeman. "There will be many others to join you, so you won't be alone. Bring food, gloves, and a shovel if you have them. Keep in mind that you will not be returning until dark tonight."

With that, the policeman left and began knocking on more doors in the Barton's neighborhood. He seemed kinder and more in control than the members of the neighborhood safety committees, so he must have been a genuine policeman.

Not every single home on the edge of town had been spared from the fire. There were some here and there that either were knocked off their foundations or burned down as well, but there were also many who had been spared. From these homes, hundreds and hundreds of men as well as teenagers were solicited to provide aid during the disaster. The women and children for the most part stayed at home to watch over the young and to help as much as they could in their own neighborhoods.

Andrew filled Angelica in on the details, and after much hesitation, she finally gave in to letting Ernie go with him. Many of the men gathering at the street corner outside were people that Andrew and Ernie knew, and they were happy to see that their friends and neighbors were all working together in this time of crisis.

"George, so good to see you made it!" said Andrew to his neighbor from down the street. "Are Mary and the rest of your family alright?"

"Yes, we were one of the lucky families, like you, "answered George McCarthy. " But we heard that Mary's sister and their family are missing, and it doesn't look good.

"Well, all we can do is pray and hope that the good Lord spared them," said Andrew. "That is exactly why we are out here now – to help people know good news or bad news. Either way, they need to know."

"Dad, I'm not sure I can do this," said Ernie. "I don't want to see any more dead people."

As Andrew looked at his young son, he couldn't help but feel very proud. Ernie had had to grow up very quickly in the last few days, and he'd seen more things than a boy his age should be allowed to see.

"Ernie, don't worry, son," said Andrew. "I'll try to handle the ugly stuff if you can just help move debris. Whatever help you can give is much appreciated. Things should be a little more calmed down now that the fire is over. Not that it is completely safe- you and I both know that- but hopefully it is safer than before. If things start to get out of hand again, I'll see if I can take you home. Your mother made me promise that, and I keep my promises."

The group of about fifty men and teens then headed toward the city in a long procession, carrying their shovels and lunch bags if they had any. They walked past several businesses who had created makeshift stores to sell whatever was left of their provisions. Canvas roofs were covering the tops of these stores, and wooden frames had been hastily assembled to hold them up. Exorbitant prices were being charged for things as basic as apples and pears, but many people were more than happy to pay them. Rich and poor, Chinese or Caucasian, all seemed to be in the same predicament, and class boundaries seemed to disappear.

"Have you heard about the folks in Golden Gate Park?" asked George as they walked along Van Ness. "Those tents they put up?"

"We saw it with our own eyes!" said Ernie.

"Well, people of all kinds are mixing together in those tents," said George. "You'll see women in fancy clothes looking like they just came from the opera house fighting over government handouts like canned corn and beans with a Chinaman or a bum off the street! It's quite something how a disaster can level the playing field, so to speak, isn't it?"

"Very true, George," said Andrew. "Money doesn't mean a whole lot when there is nowhere to spend it, and high class just goes right out the window."

"Look at that over there, Dad!" said Ernie as they continued down the street. "It looks like somebody already got some lumber and started building their home again!"

"That might turn out to be a bad idea, son," said his father. "I'm sure he is building it in quite a rush, and if there are more quakes in the future, that thing will fall like a bunch of matchsticks because it was so poorly built."

Andrew knew when things were being built correctly. He had done some construction work as a younger man, and he hated to see things put together in a shoddy manner.

"Hopefully, people will learn from all this and start to build their homes and businesses better, said George. "The last thing we need is to repeat the same mistakes of our fathers."

"Right now, what I am even more worried about are those dead bodies that are laying out on the street with nothing but a sheet over them," said Andrew, just out of Ernie's earshot.

"I hate to say it, but bubonic plague and a host of other diseases tend to spread like wildfire when these things happen."

"I'm sure the Red Cross will do what they can to avoid that," replied George. "Right now, we haven't got any choice. We either help out or they arrest us. They might even shoot us if we complain or speak out. I've seen that happening to a lot of people this week!"

"Tell me about it," said Andrew, showing him the wound that he'd received earlier from the vigilante safety committee.

"You're still out here doing this today?" queried George.

"Well, it doesn't hurt that much anymore. I just hope it doesn't happen again!" said Andrew.

"Me too, Dad!" said Ernie. "That was a close call!"

Finally, after walking several blocks, the men and boys were given their orders.

"Now listen here, boys!" said the policeman. "Start moving these bricks out to the street. Pile them up with your shovels or by hand. Form a line and pass them down, do it however you can, but we need to know if there are any survivors left here."

The building was unrecognizable to Andrew, but George told him it was the Call Building. It was hard to tell what was what in a city that looked like a bomb had been dropped on it. As the men handed one brick to another, they held out little hope that any survivors were to be found. It was extremely quiet and still.

"Dad, how can anyone still be under all this concrete?" asked Ernie.

"There probably isn't anyone alive, Ernie, but we've got to pretend for now that there might be. Just stay quiet and don't talk too much. These policemen get crazy sometimes."

Hours passed by with brick after brick and board after board. The men were sweating profusely and in dire need of water, but such a thing was quite a luxury. Only a few had any water at all and they all started to tire quickly and pant with exhaustion.

At about four o'clock that afternoon, they were all about to give in to the exhaustion when one of the boys in the group saw some hair poking through the bricks. Ernie's friend, Matthew, had been that boy.

"Look!" shouted Matthew. "Is that human hair?"

"No, it can't be," said another man. "It's probably a rat or something."

As Matthew picked up another brick, he noticed the hair moving – a small patch of gray hair.

"It's a man!" shouted Matthew.

All the men feverishly began unpiling the rubble, and they eventually exposed an older, wrinkled man, perhaps in his seventies.

"Is he breathing?" asked George.

Matthew put his head near the man's mouth. Everyone listened quietly. One could hear a pin drop it was so deathly quiet.

"Yes! He is!" cried Matthew.

To the amazement of the crowd, the man began to speak.

"Help me!" he cried. "My ribs must be broken. I can't breathe!"

Very carefully, the men pulled him out from the rubble. They placed him on a stretcher and rushed him to the nearest Red Cross clinic.

"Wow!" said Ernie. "How could he have lived through that, dad? All this time? He didn't have any water!"

"It is a miracle, Ern!" said Andrew.

"Wait!" shouted Matthew. "I think I hear something down there in the basement!"

The opening in which they had found the old man was actually a sort of window into the basement of the Call Building. The men had been working all day to unearth this opening, and it was amazing that they had saved this one man's life. Could there be more men?

"Yes! I can hear people talking!" said George. "We've got to move these bricks – now!"

The men began pouring through brick after brick once again, with a new enthusiasm and a new purpose.

"Hello! How many of you are down there?" shouted the policeman.

"Eight!" came the faint voice of a woman. "We need water! Please, get us some water!"

The policeman quickly notified his men of the situation and water was brought within minutes to the site. The men continued to make the opening bigger and bigger, until they could climb inside the basement and assess the condition of whoever was still down there. One by one, all eight people – two women and six men – were carried from the building and brought to Red Cross workers, doctors, and nurses who were eagerly waiting to help the living rather than bury the dead.

Later that afternoon, when Ernie and Andrew finally got to return home, Ernie asked his father a question that had been on his mind for some time.

"Dad, how do you suppose all eight of those people co survived like they did? The odds of that happening are pretty slim, aren't they?"

"Slim indeed, Ernie! Slim indeed. I suppose you could say that the conditions were right, that they were very healthy people, or other things like that, but I don't think it was an accident that we got to see it. I prefer to look at it as a miracle that God did for us and them at the last minute, and He alone knew how much we all needed one."

Made in the USA
San Bernardino, CA
08 March 2015